cocktails
AROUND THE world

cocktails
AROUND
THE
world

DAVID BIGGS

NEW
HOLLAND

First published in 2007 by New Holland Publishers (UK) Ltd
London • Cape Town • Sydney • Auckland

2 4 6 8 10 9 7 5 3 1

www.newhollandpublishers.com

Garfield House, 86–88 Edgware Road, London W2 2EA, UK
80 McKenzie Street, Cape Town 8001, South Africa
Unit 1, 66 Gibbes Street, Chatsworth, NSW 2067, Australia
218 Lake Road, Northcote, Auckland, New Zealand

ISBN: 978 1 84537 691 8

PUBLISHING DIRECTOR: Rosemary Wilkinson
EDITOR: Kate Parker
DESIGN AND COVER DESIGN: Casebourne Rose Design Associates
PRODUCTION: Marion Storz

Reproduction by Pica Digital Pte Ltd, Singapore
Printed and bound by Tien Wah Press (Pte) Ltd, Singapore

Note: The author and publishers have made every effort to ensure that the information given in this book is
safe and accurate, but they cannot accept liability for any resulting injury or loss or damage
to either property or person, whether direct or consequential and howsoever arising.

contents

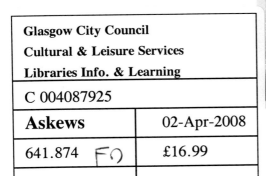

introduction

From Brazil to Bombay and from Sydney to San Francisco, cocktails are stirring up renewed interest. It's not hard to understand why this is happening. We live in an increasingly mass-produced society, where 'globalisation' is the name of the game. The same brands of cheese, chocolate and coffee appear on supermarket shelves throughout the world. There are very few old-style family-owned shops left; every little town has the same stores on the Main Street and the same products on those shelves.

And in the world of drinks, you can now get your favourite brand of beer in any bar in Paris, Perth or Port o' Spain and they taste the same wherever you go. The Cobra Beer drunk in South Africa is Indian in origin, with the company's headquarters in Britain. However, the beer is actually brewed in Poland because it is cheaper to ship from there than from England. That's globalisation.

But cocktails are different.

Although the basic ingredients of all the classic cocktails may be the same, each mixologist makes them his or her own way. The Bloody Mary you enjoy in Bangkok will be quite different from the one you had in Brisbane. Whole books have been written about the Martini, with enough variations of that single cocktail to fill hundreds of pages.

Bartenders become legends because of their special skills with the cocktail shaker. Serious cocktail connoisseurs will travel halfway round the world to taste the famous Martinis made in Tony's Bar in Rome, or the Gimlet they serve in Planet, formerly known as the Nelson's Eye, in Cape Town.

In this book we list many cocktails by country, but the language of the cocktail shaker is universal, so you are just as likely to find a Black Russian in Oslo as you are in Moscow.

What is different is that local ingredients are often used in cocktails, making them unique to that country. Shoshu, for example, is a distinctly Japanese spirit that is not used to a great extent internationally. It now appears in several Japanese drinks. The kiwano, or horned melon, is an Australian fruit, and has added its individuality to a range of exciting Aussie drinks. African drinkers enjoy an unusual cream liqueur called Marula Cream, which appears in several local cocktails.

The recipes listed here should be regarded as guidelines. The great joy of mixing cocktails lies in creating flavours that are uniquely yours. Nobody can tell you how to mix a Manhattan any more than they can tell you how to paint a picture of a cloud. These are things you must do in your own style.

Maybe the cocktail bar has become the last bastion of mankind's individuality.

the recipes

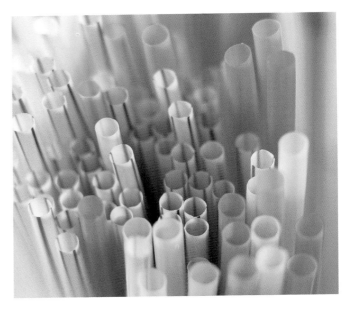

The recipes in this book are for your guidance only. Experiment with proportions: a little more here and a little less there, depending on personal taste.

Don't be afraid to add a touch of sweetness (using grenadine or sugar syrup), a hint of bitterness (using Angostura bitters) or a touch of sourness (with lemon or lime juice). Anybody can read the standard recipe for a dry martini, but it takes an inspired bartender to create a truly memorable one.

We hope these pages will provide plenty of inspiration. Remember, though, that a great cocktail is not merely a way of getting as much alcohol as possible into your guest! It should be a treat for all the senses. A good cocktail looks good, smells good and tastes wonderful. A good cocktail balances the sweet with the sour, the sticky with the astringent. And, above all, it should stimulate interesting conversation and cement lasting friendships.

Cocktail recipes vary from bar to bar and this is as it should be. Every good bartender has his or her own recipes for classic cocktails. There are no 'right' or 'wrong' ways of making a drink, as long as it's the one you enjoy.

Some bartenders have the knack of finding exactly the right proportions to suit their particular customers. This is what makes them great.

In these chapters, you will find recipes for cocktails containing brandy, whisky, vodka, gin, rum and wine, as well as some of the new and exciting varieties of drink available.

the measures

In this book we have tried to avoid using actual quantities when recording cocktail recipes. The reason for this is that almost every country has its own set of measurements. Some bartenders use gills, others use fluid ounces and still others measure their drinks in centilitres. If we had used conversions (take 2 oz/6 cl) the book would have become rather clumsy and confusing to the reader.

It's far easier to work in proportion, we believe. 'One part' of vodka to 'two parts of orange juice' will taste just the same whether the parts are teaspoons, tot measures or jugs. By using proportions rather than quantities you can decide on the size of your drinks and also make up more than one at a time by substituting a coffee mug (or a bucket!) for your usual bar measuring jigger.

famous bars

The cocktail is an American invention (now enjoyed in almost every country), so it's not surprising that good cocktail bars will usually be found wherever Americans gather to drink, at home or abroad.

During the American Prohibition era many sophisticated Americans enjoyed the freedom of travelling in Europe, where they could relax and imbibe alcoholic drinks without having to glance over their shoulders to see whether a stern police officer was taking down their names. Paris, Rome, Venice and other European capitals became the gathering places of the American intellectual crowd abroad, and where they went, cocktails followed.

It's an odd coincidence that two of the world's most famous cocktail bars are called 'Harry's', but there's no direct connection between Harry's New York Bar in Paris and Harry's Bar in Venice. Their stories are fascinating.

Harry's New York Bar in Paris was founded by Harry MacElhone and became the meeting place of Americans living in Paris in the 1920s. Not only could they enjoy the imaginative cocktails from Harry's shaker, but it was one of the few places in France that served a good old American-style hot dog. Many cocktail classics, such as the Sidecar, have been attributed to Harry's inventive genius.

George Gershwin is alleged to have picked out the tune of 'An American in Paris' while sitting at the downstairs piano of Harry's New York Bar.

Above: Rich and elegant, the best cocktails bars are lavishly designed to attract the world's glitterati. Pictured is the King Cole Bar in The St. Regis Hotel, New York.
Opposite: The Martini comes in an almost infinite variety of forms; this '1763' Martini is a favourite of many drinkers.

Gertrude Stein jotted down her poetry on Harry's tablecloths. Ernest Hemingway and F. Scott Fitzgerald were regulars.

It was in this famous bar that Fernand Petiot, one of the bartenders, invented the Bloody Mary, starting a whole new family of spicy cocktails. Today the Bloody Mary is said to be the most popular vodka-based drink in America.

The other Harry's Bar was founded in kindness. A young American playboy, Harry Pickering, was living in Venice with his delightful maiden aunt and her gigolo. Frankly, she was a lot more fun than Harry's rather stuffy parents. The three were regular customers at the bar of the Hotel Europa,

where Giuseppe Cipriani wielded the magic cocktail shaker. After several months of happy and regular drinking, Harry suddenly stopped coming in for drinks.

One day Giuseppe met him and asked what was the matter. Was he ill? Did he no longer like the drinks at the Europa?

It turned out that Harry's parents had discovered he was living the high life of a playboy and had cut off his allowance. Suddenly he was broke.

Giuseppe advanced him $5000, a vast sum in those days, and Harry returned to America.

Two years later he returned to the Europa a wealthy man and repaid Giuseppe with liberal interest and a substantial cash gift in gratitude for his loan. With the money, Giuseppe was able to leave the Europa and start his own bar in what had been a rope warehouse. He named it 'Harry's Bar' in honour of the young American who had made it possible. Today, the bar is run by

Giuseppe's son, named Arrigo by parents who knew he would one day be in charge of Harry's. It must be the only instance in the world of a child being named after the bar he would one day own.

In 1934, after Prohibition had ended in America, the famous Petiot of Harry's New York Bar in Paris accepted an invitation to become the head barman at the Regis Hotel in New York. In due course the Regis Bar became almost as famous as Harry's had been.

Other bars that have enjoyed their moments of cocktail glory with the world's rich and famous include the Ritz in Paris, the American Bar at the Savoy in London and the Long Bar at Raffles Hotel in Singapore.

And while the glitterati were enjoying the cocktail lifestyle in Europe, things were by no means dull in America. When Prohibition ended in 1933, the social action shifted from shady speakeasies to more glamorous nightclubs like the Stork Club, the El Morocco, Park Avenue Club and Morgan's.

Of course, cocktail bars are only as renowned as their bartenders, and the cocktail crowd tended to drift to where the best cocktails were reputed to be served. This is still the case today.

Opposite: The American Bar at The Savoy in London was opened by a bartender fleeing Prohibition in the 1930s.

Right: The earthy decor of the two-storey Long Bar – home of the Singapore Sling (page 206) – at Raffles Hotel in Singapore was inspired by Malayan plantations in the 1920s.

stocking up

There are literally thousands of alcoholic drinks available to the enthusiastic bartender and nobody can be expected to stock every one of them, but as you increase your repertoire of cocktails, you'll wish to add new and different drinks to your stock.

Every bar should have a basic range of spirits, mixers and garnishes, which can be adapted to suit your own needs.

We have not listed wines in any detail here, because wine is a vast subject that fills many books on its own. For the basic cocktail bar you should have a dry white wine and a serviceable red blend.

Here's a list of basics to act as a guide for the beginner bartender.

The spirits

Brandy or cognac

Gin

Vodka

Rum (dark and light)

Scotch whisky

Bourbon

Tequila

Vermouth, dry and sweet

Dry sparkling wine

Dry white wine (Sauvignon Blanc is a safe bet)

Dry red wine (an inexpensive blended red wine will do)

Triple Sec

Your own choice of liqueurs

The mixers

Club soda
Cola
Ginger ale
Indian tonic water
Tomato juice
Fruit juices
Mineral water
Grenadine
Angostura bitters

Lemons
Limes
Oranges
Nutmeg
Caster sugar
Tabasco sauce
Worcestershire sauce
Sugar syrup (gomme)
Sour syrup (a mixture of lemon
    and lime juice)

Sauces, spices and garnishes

Maraschino cherries
Olives (green and black)
Cocktail onions

And finally...

Ice, ice and more ice: cubes, crushed and cracked.
You can never have too much ice in a good
cocktail bar.

equipment

For many readers, cocktails will be a passing fancy – a one-party stand – and there's nothing wrong with that. If this is what you are doing you'll probably find all the equipment you need already in your home. You can use ordinary kitchen tools and utensils to create almost any cocktail.

But for those who wish to take their cocktail making a little more seriously, it's worth getting a few accessories that will make your task much more enjoyable and certainly enhance your reputation as a host.

When selecting equipment, always try to buy high-quality items. They should look good, feel good and do the job for which they are designed.

Here's a short list of items the budding home bartender would need:

Sharp knife

Ice bucket: The traditional ice bucket is made of metal, but in hot climates it might be better to have one with an insulated lining.

Ice tongs

Measure: It doesn't really matter what size measure you use, as long as you use the same one for all the ingredients of your drink; they are also known as 'jiggers' or 'tot measures'.

It may be a good idea to have two measures, one with twice the capacity of the other.

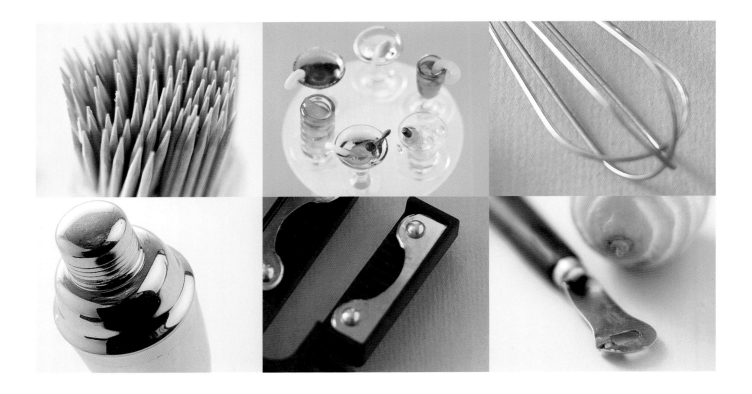

Corkscrews: There are many different kinds available. There is the 'screwpull' range, which has the spirals with a non-stick coating; the 'waiter's friend', which has an arm that rests on the rim of the bottle to provide leverage; the 'wing' corkscrew, which has two arms that are depressed to lift the cork from the bottle neck; the 'Ah So', which is a cork lifter rather than a corkscrew, with two slender prongs of spring steel that are slid down the sides of the cork and then carefully twisted out (it is designed to handle corks that have become crumbly with age); and the 'cork pump', a hand-operated pump attached to a hollow needle, which is pushed down through the cork.

Bottle opener
Cocktail shaker
Bar glass with strainer
Water pitcher

The following are useful if mixing drinks in substantial quantities:

Bar spoon
Cloths
Bar towels
Damp wiping cloth

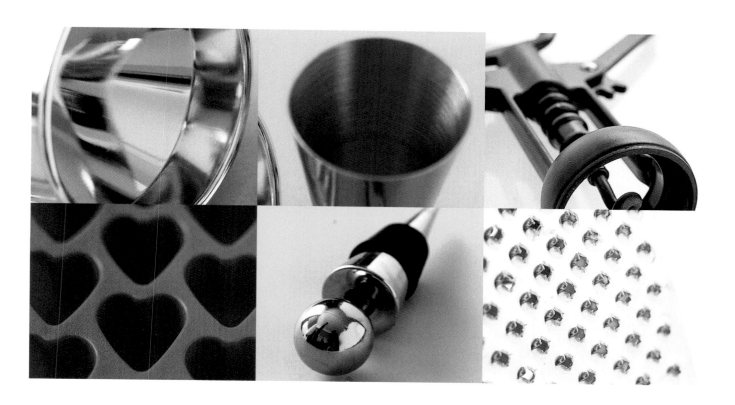

glasses

Cocktail purists will throw up their hands in horror if they see a drink being served in the 'wrong' kind of glass. Martinis, they will tell you, should be served only in martini glasses, and a Harvey Wallbanger in anything but a highball glass would be a mortal sin. In today's more relaxed age, however, we tend to be less rigid about our choice of glasses.

There's a wide range of glasses available for cocktails and it probably isn't necessary to have sets of all of them in your cocktail bar. For all practical purposes you should get by with just four designs – the highball, the low-ball, the champagne flute and the cocktail glass. One of the basic guidelines is that the stronger the drink, the smaller the glass.

The shot glass (1)
This small glass is used to serve a drink with a very high alcohol content, and for those colourful little 'shooters' that are meant to be downed in a single, throat-searing gulp.

The cocktail glass (2)
This is an elegant little glass with a shallow, flared bowl, and a stem to prevent your hand warming the chilled drink too much.

The martini glass (3)
Probably the best known and most often photographed of all cocktail glasses, it is used for martinis and margaritas.

The brandy balloon (4)
Designed to provide the brandy in it with a very large surface area to allow the aroma to rise, it has a rather narrow mouth to gather the bouquet and concentrate it for maximum impact.

Port and sherry glasses (5)

These miniature wineglasses are designed to take a small amount of fortified wine.

The champagne saucer (6)

Totally impractical for champagne, as it allows the bubbles to dissipate too quickly, it is suitable for certain cocktails such as Russian Coffee (page 168). If you do happen to have some of these old-fashioned glasses, don't toss them out. They come in handy as elegant servers for nuts and bar nibbles.

The champagne flute (7)

This elegantly slim glass is perfect for any champagne-based drink, or, in fact, anything with bubbles in it. The tall, clear glass shows off the bubbles to best effect as they rise slowly up the column, and the small surface area ensures that the bubbles do not disappear too fast.

The lowball glass (8)

This is often used for Bloody Marys and other drinks that have a large proportion of mixer to alcohol.

The highball glass (9)

This taller version of the lowball glass is intended for long drinks like fruit punches and Harvey Wallbangers.

The Paris goblet (10)

This is the standard wineglass, which is also used for drinks like pink gin. In most home bars where there is not a wide range of glassware, the Paris goblet doubles up happily as an alternate cocktail or martini glass.

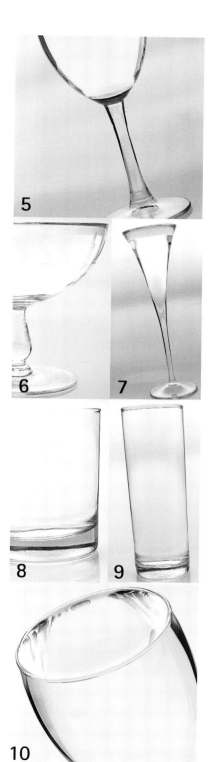

decorating your drink

One of the charming things about cocktails is that they are designed to please all the senses. They should not only taste good but smell good and look good as well. And the tinkle of ice in a glass is certainly a wonderful sound.

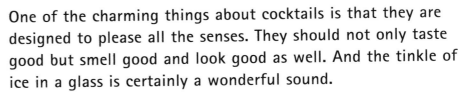

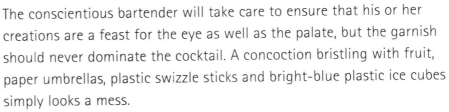

The conscientious bartender will take care to ensure that his or her creations are a feast for the eye as well as the palate, but the garnish should never dominate the cocktail. A concoction bristling with fruit, paper umbrellas, plastic swizzle sticks and bright-blue plastic ice cubes simply looks a mess.

By adding just the right touch of garnish, however, a clever bartender can give an indication of the flavour to be expected. A twist of lemon or lime, for example, tells the drinker to be prepared for a crisp, slightly tangy drink. A maraschino cherry on a cocktail stick or a ball of pink watermelon would indicate something sweet and syrupy.

Some garnishes, like a sprig of mint, actually add to the flavour or aroma of the drink, while there are certain cocktails that traditionally include a specific garnish, like the olive in a dry martini.

A pretty touch can be added by serving the cocktail in a glass with a frosted rim. This is usually done by wetting the rim of the glass, either with water or egg white, and then dipping it carefully into a saucer of fine sugar; the sugar sticks to the moistened edge.

In the case of a margarita, the rim of the glass is traditionally frosted with salt.

Some drinks are best sipped through a straw, and unless the glass is a tall one, a short straw is best. Trim off as much of a full-length straw as you require.

The role of fruit

Many cocktail recipes call for fruit, and even some of those that don't can be enhanced by the addition of a slice of fresh fruit dropped into the glass, or a chunk threaded onto a cocktail stick, if the mood is right.

Fruit can play a number of roles in the creation of the perfect cocktail for the occasion. And it is also ideal for adding visual attractiveness.

Appropriate fruits, when in season, can provide an exciting base for a cocktail. Bananas, melons, peaches, apricots and all sorts of soft fruit can be liquidized in a blender to create a delicious fruit purée. Vodka, rum or brandy added to it gives you a superb drink.

Use the pictures on these pages to provide you with inspiration when you're creating a new drink.

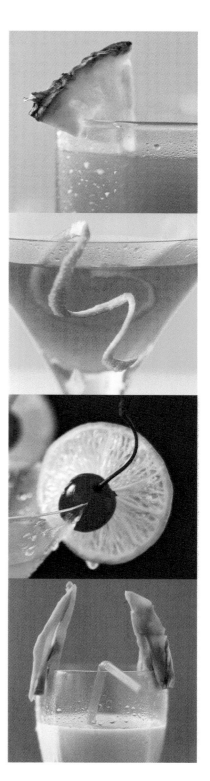

north america

North America is the home of the cocktail, ironically because of the bleak years of Prohibition in the USA, designed to stamp out 'the demon' alcohol. The sale of alcohol was illegal, so many backroom distilleries produced crude versions, so revolting they needed added ingredients. The cocktail was the result.

Prairie Oyster

Some claim the Prairie Oyster is one of America's great inventions, offering an almost instant hangover cure. You do have to be brave to face one after a heavy night's imbibing, though, and for some the idea is just too daunting. Traditionally, this concoction should be downed in a single gulp – you're welcome to try it.

ICE CUBES

ONE GENEROUS MEASURE OF BRANDY

TWO TEASPOONS OF CIDER VINEGAR

A DESSERTSPOON OF WORCESTERSHIRE SAUCE

A TEASPOON OF TOMATO SAUCE (KETCHUP)

HALF A TEASPOON OF ANGOSTURA BITTERS

THE YOLK OF A FRESH EGG

CAYENNE PEPPER

❏ Place five ice cubes in a cocktail shaker and add the brandy, vinegar, Worcestershire sauce, tomato sauce and bitters.

❏ Shake well and strain into a lowball glass, adding ice cubes to bring the drink to the top of the glass.

❏ Carefully float the unbroken yolk of the egg on top of the drink and sprinkle it lightly with cayenne pepper.

Stinger

This very old cocktail recipe has its origins in the days of American Prohibition and has become a true classic. Originally it was served 'straight up' but most people now prefer to sip it on the rocks. It's a good way to get a party rolling as fast as possible; one or two Stingers and your guests are almost guaranteed to be in a jolly mood.

ICE CUBES

TWO PARTS BRANDY

ONE PART WHITE CRÈME DE MENTHE

❏ Place six ice cubes in a cocktail shaker and add the brandy and crème de menthe.

❏ Shake well and strain into a chilled cocktail glass.

❏ Serve ungarnished or with a sprig of mint.

Opposite: The clean, minty flavour of the Stinger makes it a superb drink to serve before or at the end of a good meal.

Above: The Charleston was named after one of the most popular dances during the Prohibition era.

Charleston

The Charleston was one of the most popular dances during the Prohibition era and typified the new, rather risqué age, when young ladies could show an ankle in public and dresses were figure-hugging and sheer rather than elaborate and all-concealing. This drink would have appealed to the liberated young women of the time. It appeals just as much today.

ONE PART MANDARIN NAPOLEON LIQUEUR

ONE PART CHERRY BRANDY

ICE CUBES

LEMONADE TO TASTE

○ Place the mandarin Napoleon and cherry brandy in a bar glass and stir well.

○ Pour over a highball glass full of ice cubes.

○ Top up with lemonade and serve.

Above: A sweeter version of this classic cocktail, Bronx, can be made by substituting some or all of the dry vermouth with sweet vermouth.

Bronx

In the wild days of Prohibition, a different gang boss controlled each area of a city, and booze played an important role in the economy of the underworld. Different areas of New York became known for the special drinks they offered. This was the speciality of the Bronx.

The secondary ingredients were probably a desperate attempt to disguise the taste of the homemade bathtub gin. Modern gin, however, turns it into an elegant treat.

ICE CUBES
THREE PARTS GIN
ONE PART FRESH ORANGE JUICE
ONE PART DRY VERMOUTH

○ Place four or five ice cubes in a cocktail shaker. Add the gin, orange juice and vermouth and shake well.

○ Strain into a cocktail glass and serve.

Above: The egg white added to the Rattlesnake gives it its silky texture.

Right: An early label from the Jack Daniel Distillery, which in 1866 became the first registered distillery in America.

Rattlesnake

One of the many slang names for illicit moonshine liquor was 'snake juice', which probably referred to the rough mountain-distilled spirit. This is a refined version, using bourbon.

CRUSHED ICE

TWO PARTS BOURBON

ONE TEASPOON OF LEMON JUICE

ONE TEASPOON OF SUGAR SYRUP

HALF AN EGG WHITE

SEVERAL DASHES OF PERNOD

○ Place a scoop of crushed ice in a cocktail shaker and add the bourbon, lemon juice, sugar syrup, egg white and Pernod.

○ Shake vigorously for 10 seconds or more and strain into a chilled lowball glass.

○ Serve ungarnished.

Above: Widow's Kiss is a potent brew of applejack and Benedictine, which sets one wondering what happened to the widow's late husband.

Widow's Kiss

The spirit distilled from apple cider in the New England area of America is known as applejack. It is more or less the same as Calvados from France and has a hefty alcohol content of about 45 per cent.

CRUSHED ICE

ONE PART APPLEJACK

ONE PART BENEDICTINE

HALF A PART YELLOW CHARTREUSE

A DASH OF ANGOSTURA BITTERS

A FRESH STRAWBERRY

○ Place a scoop of crushed ice in a cocktail shaker and add the applejack, Benedictine, chartreuse and bitters.

○ Shake well, strain into a chilled cocktail glass and float the fresh strawberry on the top.

Aviation Spirit

Probably not strong enough to use as aircraft fuel, this is apparently a favourite drink in the bars of some US Air Force bases. Maybe the 'spirit' part refers to the camaraderie among pilots.

ICE CUBES

TWO PARTS GIN

ONE PART FRESH LEMON JUICE

TWO DASHES OF MARASCHINO

○ Place four or five ice cubes in a cocktail shaker, add the gin, lemon and maraschino and shake well.

○ Strain into a chilled cocktail glass and serve.

Left: The tangy drink called Aviation Spirit has kept American pilots' spirits soaring in USAF bases around the world.

Fare Thee Well

This is an interesting variation on the classic Martini theme, with added flavour for those who are tired of too-dry drinks.

ICE CUBES

ONE PART GIN

ONE PART DRY VERMOUTH

A SPLASH OF COINTREAU

A SPLASH OF SWEET VERMOUTH

○ Place five or six ice cubes in a cocktail shaker, add all the ingredients and shake well.

○ Strain into a cocktail glass and serve ungarnished.

Right: Fare Thee Well offers a sweet farewell drink to end a friendly evening.

Above: This little drink is as smooth and debonair as the great movie hero after which it may have been named.

Fairbanks Cocktail

Possibly named after the swashbuckling hero of early Hollywood adventure films, Douglas Fairbanks, this is a good cocktail to sip while watching re-runs of old movies.

ICE CUBES

FOUR PARTS RYE WHISKEY

ONE PART APRICOT BRANDY

DASH OF ANGOSTURA BITTERS

SLICE OF APRICOT

○ Place five or six ice cubes in a bar glass, add the ingredients and stir until well mixed.

○ Strain into a lowball glass, garnish with the apricot slice and serve.

Tom and Jerry

This classic cocktail is not actually named after the famous cartoon cat and mouse duo. It was invented way back in the 1850s by one Jerry Thomas, called 'The Professor', in his famous Planter's House bar in St Louis, Missouri. The name later came to change from Jerry Thomas to Tom and Jerry.

ONE EGG

HALF A PART SUGAR SYRUP (OR LESS TO TASTE)

ONE PART DARK JAMAICAN RUM

ONE PART COGNAC

BOILING WATER

GRATED NUTMEG

○ Separate the yolk of the egg from the white and beat each separately.

○ Fold them together and add the sugar syrup.

○ Place this mixture in a warmed coffee mug, add the rum and cognac and top up with boiling water.

○ Sprinkle grated nutmeg on top and serve piping hot.

Left: Tom and Jerry is a rum-based cocktail reputed to cure the common cold – or help you forget its misery!

Martha Washington

We don't know whether Martha actually drank this, but it certainly helps keep her name alive.

TWO PARTS RYE OR BOURBON WHISKEY

ONE PART CHERRY LIQUEUR

A SPLASH OF ORANGE JUICE TO TASTE

CRUSHED ICE

A MARASCHINO CHERRY

○ Mix all the liquid ingredients with crushed ice in a blender or cocktail shaker and strain into a cocktail glass.

○ Garnish with the cherry.

Apricot Pie

Fruit is plentiful in California, so it's natural to combine the apricot flavours with easily obtainable citrus. And in the land of the martini, every bar is stocked with vermouth.

CRUSHED ICE

ONE PART LIGHT RUM

ONE PART SWEET VERMOUTH

ONE TEASPOON APRICOT BRANDY OR TO TASTE

ONE TEASPOON FRESH LEMON JUICE OR TO TASTE

ONE TEASPOON GRENADINE OR TO TASTE

ORANGE PEEL TO GARNISH

○ Place a generous scoop of crushed ice in a cocktail shaker or a blender and add the rum, sweet vermouth, apricot brandy, lemon juice and grenadine.

○ Shake or blend well and strain into a chilled cocktail glass.

○ Twist the orange peel over the drink to release the zest, then drop it in as decoration.

Left: Rye and Bourbon whiskey are about as American as you can get, as was Martha Washinton, who gave her name to this drink.

Harvey Wallbanger

The story behind the intriguing name of this drink is that Harvey was a surfer who was eliminated in a surfing championship in California. He was so angry at his defeat that he headed for Pancho's Bar at Manhattan Beach and soothed his bruised ego by drinking a large quantity of vodka and Galliano. He then banged his head against a wall and urged his friends to take him home and stop his destructive drinking.

Whether it's true or not, the name has stuck and the drink is a firm favourite throughout the world.

ICE CUBES

TWO PARTS VODKA

FIVE PARTS FRESH ORANGE JUICE

ONE PART GALLIANO

A SLICE OF ORANGE

○ Place four or five ice cubes in a cocktail shaker and add the vodka and orange juice.

○ Shake well and strain into a highball glass.

○ Add two ice cubes and gently float the Galliano on top.

○ Garnish with a slice of orange on the rim of the glass and serve with a straw.

Above: The Harvey Wallbanger – a frustrated surfer's gift to the world of cocktails.

Nob Hill

You can play with the balance between sweet and sour here, to reach your perfect palate cleanser.

TWO PARTS RYE WHISKEY

ONE PART GRAPEFRUIT JUICE

HONEY TO TASTE

ICE CUBES

○ Place the ingredients in a cocktail shaker with a handful of ice cubes; shake well and strain into a cocktail glass.

○ Serve ungarnished.

Kay Biscayne

The elegant white lighthouse at Kay Biscayne on the Florida Keys has guided sailors home for many years. Maybe this typical American drink was designed to celebrate a safe journey home from a party.

THREE PARTS BOURBON WHISKEY

ONE PART CURAÇAO

ONE PART SWEET VERMOUTH

JUICE OF HALF A LIME

CRUSHED ICE

A SPRIG OF MINT

○ Add all the ingredients, except the mint, to crushed ice in a cocktail shaker.

○ Shake well and strain into a chilled cocktail glass.

○ Decorate with a sprig of mint.

Left: An elegant little drink to serve in sophisticated company, the Nob Hill combines sweet and sour to perfection.

Opposite: The Kay Biscayne is named after a picturesque lighthouse on one of Florida's famous Keys.

New Orleans

Many cocktails take their names from the places where they were invented. This one obviously originated in the southern United States and evokes images of the Mardi Gras and Dixieland jazz.

CRUSHED ICE

THREE PARTS BOURBON

ONE PART PERNOD

THREE DASHES OF ANGOSTURA BITTERS

A DASH OF ANISETTE

A TEASPOON OF SUGAR SYRUP (OR LESS TO TASTE)

ICE CUBES

A TWIST OF LEMON

○ Place a scoop of crushed ice in a cocktail shaker and add the bourbon, Pernod, bitters, anisette and sugar syrup.

○ Shake vigorously and strain into a lowball glass filled with ice cubes. Garnish with a twist of lemon before serving.

Above: New Orleans is a tangy and complex array of flavours.

Comfortable Screw

Southern Comfort is a delicious orange-and-peach-flavoured whiskey produced in the southern United States.

ICE CUBES

ONE PART SOUTHERN COMFORT

SIX PARTS FRESH ORANGE JUICE

A BANANA

❍ Place six ice cubes in a cocktail shaker and add the Southern Comfort and orange juice.

❍ Shake well and strain into a lowball glass.

❍ Garnish with the banana and serve.

Above: The Comfortable Screw gets its rather naughty name from the fact that it is a Screwdriver made with Southern Comfort instead of vodka.

The Blue Arrow

From New Orleans, home of the Blues, comes this tribute to one of America's greatest music genres. In the normal course of events, we hardly ever eat or drink anything that is blue, so this colourful drink immediately conjures up visions of something new and exciting.

CRUSHED ICE

TWO PARTS GIN

ONE PART COINTREAU

ONE PART LIME JUICE CORDIAL

ONE PART BLUE CURAÇAO

○ Place about two cups of crushed ice in a cocktail shaker.

○ Pour in the gin, Cointreau, lime juice and blue Curaçao and shake vigorously for about five seconds.

○ Strain into a chilled cocktail glass and serve ungarnished.

Left: Blue drinks have an exciting aura. Try the Blue Arrow and capture some of the mystery.

Golden Cadillac

Galliano has a vivid golden colour and a nutty-sweet flavour. The crème de cacao gives a smooth chocolaty flavour and the cream allows it to slip down like liquid velvet.

ICE CUBES

ONE PART GALLIANO

ONE PART CRÈME DE CACAO

ONE PART THIN CREAM

○ Place three ice cubes in a cocktail shaker and add the Galliano, crème de cacao and cream.

○ Shake well and strain into a cocktail glass.

○ Serve ungarnished.

Above: Like the limousine it was named after, the Golden Cadillac is a slick and smooth creation.

Left: Mint Julep originated in the United States' Deep South in the days of the cotton barons and Mississippi steamboats.

Opposite: Planters' Punch is an elegant reminder of the grand lifestyles at America's Southern mansions.

Mint Julep

This drink reeks of good living in an age when there were slaves and servants available at the flick of a finger to do the bidding of their master.

A good Mint Julep is a drink for the wealthy. Not many people today will be able to afford the 'tankard of bourbon' that forms the basis of the drink. But for those occasions when you do feel like a millionaire, here's the recipe.

CRUSHED ICE

A TANKARD OF BOURBON

A TEASPOON OF CASTER SUGAR

TWO TABLESPOONS OF WATER

A TEASPOON OF BARBADOS RUM

A LARGE BUNCH OF FRESHLY PICKED MINT

○ Place a cup of crushed ice in a pitcher and add the bourbon, caster sugar, water and rum. Stir well.

○ Crush the mint leaves lightly to release the flavour and place them in a serving jug.

○ Strain the contents of the bar glass into the jug, add four or five ice cubes and serve in lowball glasses.

Planters' Punch

Almost every bartender has his own version of this refreshing drink. Some add sugar while others like a dash of Maraschino in the mixture. Here's a basic recipe to use as the starting point for your own version.

CRUSHED ICE

ONE PART DARK RUM

TWO PARTS FRESH ORANGE JUICE

JUICE OF HALF A FRESH LIME OR LEMON

ONE TEASPOON CASTER SUGAR

A DASH OF GRENADINE OR GOMME SYRUP

A MARASCHINO CHERRY

○ Place about a cup of crushed ice in a cocktail shaker.

○ Add the rum, orange juice, lime or lemon juice, sugar, and grenadine or gomme syrup.

○ Shake very well and strain into a chilled lowball glass.

○ Serve decorated with the cherry on a stick.

THE MARTINI IS BY FAR the most famous cocktail in the world; long before James Bond declared it should be 'shaken, not stirred', it was a legend in the world of liquor. It is also the most versatile; whole books have been written about the many varieties of martinis – amazing for a drink that traditionally contains only two ingredients.

Dry Martini

The Dry Martini is undoubtedly the most famous cocktail in the world and every bartender has a favourite way of making it. This is just one of many martini variations.

ICE CUBES

ONE PART GIN

ONE PART DRY VERMOUTH

A GREEN OLIVE

○ Place four ice cubes in a bar glass and add the gin and dry vermouth.

○ Stir, then strain into a martini glass.

○ Garnish with the olive on a cocktail stick.

Sweet Martini

Although the Dry Martini is considered the most sophisticated, the Sweet Martini has a friendly charm of its own.

ICE CUBES

ONE PART GIN

ONE PART SWEET VERMOUTH

A COCKTAIL CHERRY

○ Place eight ice cubes in a cocktail mixing glass.

○ Add the gin and sweet vermouth.

○ Stir well and strain into a martini glass.

○ Garnish with the cocktail cherry on a cocktail stick.

Medium Martini

If you use the same measure, this one will end up rather more alcoholic than the other two. Traditionally, this elegant cocktail is served without any garnish.

ICE CUBES
ONE PART GIN
ONE PART DRY VERMOUTH
ONE PART SWEET VERMOUTH

○ Place eight ice cubes in a cocktail mixing glass and pour the gin and both measures of vermouth over them.

○ Stir well and strain into a martini glass.

Above from left to right: Dry Martini, Medium Martini, Sweet Martini. Martinis come in many forms – the difference is usually in the sweetness of the vermouth and the right choice of garnish.

Champagne Blues

This rather dramatic-looking drink was first created by American barman and author John J. Poister as a tribute to the authors of *Champagne Blues,* Nan and Ivan Lyons. They say it is impossible to have the blues when drinking champagne, so maybe we should all take note of this as a remedy for depression.

DRY CHAMPAGNE

BLUE CURAÇAO

LEMON PEEL

○ Pour the chilled champagne into a cooled tulip glass and add the blue Curaçao to taste.

○ Twist the lemon peel over the drink to release the zest and drop it into the glass as a garnish.

Above: Champagne Blues is a classic, champagne-based cocktail.

Right: The Wedding Belle was originally designed to toast a pretty bride.

The Wedding Belle

This is a pretty cocktail with which to toast the bride at a lavish reception in the grounds of a Southern mansion.

CRUSHED ICE

ONE PART GIN

ONE PART DUBONNET ROUGE

HALF A PART CHERRY BRANDY

ONE PART FRESH ORANGE JUICE

○ Place two tablespoons of crushed ice in a cocktail shaker, add the gin, Dubonnet, cherry brandy and orange juice and shake well.

○ Strain into a cocktail glass and serve.

Southern Champagne

Sparkling wine is the basis for many exciting cocktails. The 'champagne' mentioned in the recipe is probably from California, where they still call their sparkling wines by the French name.

A DASH OR TWO OF ANGOSTURA BITTERS

ONE SHOT GLASS OF SOUTHERN COMFORT

CHAMPAGNE

ORANGE PEEL

○ Splash the Angostura bitters into a champagne flute and swirl it about to coat the inside.

○ Pour in the Southern Comfort and top up with chilled champagne. Do not stir.

○ Twist a length of orange peel over the drink to release the zest and then drop the peel in as a garnish.

Right: Southern Champagne, another classic, champagne-based cocktail.

manhattan

MANHATTAN IS THE THROBBING, SOPHISTICATED HEART of New York, so it is not surprising that there's a range of elegant cocktails named after it. Like all great cocktails, the Manhattan has a variety of incarnations.

Manhattan

Like so many of life's great pleasures, the classic Manhattan cocktail is one of the simplest. To make a Dry Manhattan, substitute dry vermouth for the sweet vermouth.

CRUSHED ICE

THREE PARTS BLENDED WHISKEY

ONE PART SWEET VERMOUTH

A MARASCHINO CHERRY

○ Fill a mixing glass with crushed ice, add the whiskey and vermouth and stir well.

○ Strain into a cocktail glass and garnish with the cherry.

Brandy Manhattan

The Brandy Manhattan has become a classic because it creates the perfect balance between sweet and sour flavours. What's more, it is easily adjusted to suit individual palates; simply add a little more – or less – bitters.

ICE CUBES

FOUR PARTS BRANDY

ONE PART SWEET VERMOUTH

A DASH OF ANGOSTURA BITTERS

A MARASCHINO CHERRY

○ Place four ice cubes in a bar glass and add the brandy, vermouth and bitters.

○ Stir well, then strain into a chilled cocktail glass

○ Decorate with the maraschino cherry on a cocktail stick.

Opposite: The Manhattan – traditional drink of sophisticated New York.

Above: An elegant drink from the cream of America's intellectuals.

Harvard

Obviously, the Harvard originated at the famous American university. Perhaps it was the result of many years of learned research by earnest professors? We suspect this was not the case.

ICE CUBES

ONE PART BRANDY

HALF A TEASPOON OF SUGAR

ONE PART SWEET VERMOUTH

A DASH OF ANGOSTURA BITTERS

A SLICE OF LEMON

○ Place four ice cubes in a cocktail shaker and add the brandy, sugar and sweet vermouth.

○ Shake well.

○ Splash a dash of bitters into a cocktail glass and swirl it around to coat the sides evenly.

○ Strain the cocktail from the shaker into the glass and decorate with a slice of lemon.

New Yorker

It's hard to say whether this drink was named after the city or the magazine of the same name. Whichever it is, the drink has an air of cool sophistication and balance.

CRUSHED ICE

THREE PARTS WHISKEY

ONE PART LIME JUICE (FRESH IF POSSIBLE)

HALF A TEASPOON OF CASTER SUGAR

A DASH OF GRENADINE

A TWIST OF ORANGE

○ Place a cup of crushed ice in a cocktail shaker and add the whiskey, lime juice, sugar and grenadine.

○ Shake well and strain into a chilled cocktail glass.

○ Decorate with a twist of orange.

Above: The New Yorker offers everything that a great cocktail should – good flavour, good balance and elegance.

cosmopolitan

SOME DRINKERS CLAIM the Cosmopolitan is related to the Martini. We feel the link is tenuous; this is a drink with a personality all its own. What's more, it's likely to attract a growing number of enthusiasts as cranberry juice gains in popularity all over the world as the perfect health drink.

ICE CUBES
TWO PARTS VODKA
ONE PART COINTREAU
ONE PART CRANBERRY JUICE
ONE PART FRESH LIME JUICE
A TWIST OF LIME

○ Place four or five ice cubes in a cocktail shaker and add all the liquid ingredients.

○ Shake well and strain into a cocktail glass.

○ Garnish with a twist of lime and serve.

Opposite: The Cosmopolitan – combining flavour and health.

Bloody Mary

Although originally created in Paris, if the legend is true, the Bloody Mary has become as American as the Stars and Stripes. It must have taken some courage to create the first one. It needs imagination to blend two such disparate drinks as fiery, crystal-clear vodka and thick, slightly lumpy tomato juice; but there's no doubt it works, whatever way you make it. Here's a starter recipe.

ICE CUBES

TWO PARTS VODKA

SIX PARTS TOMATO JUICE

A TEASPOON OF TOMATO SAUCE (KETCHUP)

A DASH OF WORCESTERSHIRE SAUCE

A DASH OF TABASCO SAUCE

A PINCH OF CELERY SALT

A STICK OF CELERY

A DUSTING OF GROUND WHITE PEPPER

○ Place four ice cubes in a cocktail shaker and add the vodka and tomato juice.

○ Add the tomato sauce, Worcestershire sauce, Tabasco sauce and celery salt.

○ Shake well and strain into a highball glass.

○ Serve decorated with a stick of celery.

○ Finish with a light dusting of white pepper. (You could use black pepper, but it looks very unappetising, rather like cigar ash on the surface of the drink.)

The Waldorf Cocktail

By using different blends of whiskey you can create a whole range of different Waldorf cocktails. Traditionally, bourbon is used.

CRUSHED ICE

TWO PARTS BOURBON

ONE PART PERNOD

ONE PART SWEET VERMOUTH

A DASH OF ANGOSTURA BITTERS

○ Place a scoop of crushed ice in a bar glass and add the bourbon, Pernod, sweet vermouth and Angostura bitters.

○ Stir well, strain into a chilled cocktail glass and serve.

Above: The Waldorf Cocktail is traditionally made with bourbon rather than Scotch whisky.

Calypso Cocktail

This is a simple but delicious long drink, perfect for a long, leisurely day on a Caribbean beach beneath swaying palms. The tinkle of the ice cubes could be the echoes of calypso music.

ICE CUBES

ONE PART ORANGE CURAÇAO

GINGER ALE

A SLICE OF LEMON

○ Fill a highball glass with ice cubes, pour in the orange Curaçao and top up with enough ginger ale to fill the glass.

○ Decorate with a slice of lemon and serve.

Left: The gentle tinkle of ice cubes adds to the dream of lazy days spent listening to lapping waves on a beach.

Banana Punch

Here is the ideal drink to serve to friends at a Hawaiian sunset beach party. This tropical treat uses three kinds of fruit flavour to create a jungle taste.

CRUSHED ICE

ONE PART VODKA

ONE PART APRICOT BRANDY

THE JUICE OF HALF A LIME

SODA WATER

A SLICED BANANA

A SPRIG OF FRESH MINT

○ Place a scoop of crushed ice in a cocktail shaker and add the vodka, apricot brandy and lime juice.

○ Shake well and strain into a highball glass.

○ Top up with soda water and decorate with slices of banana and the mint.

Right: Banana punch, one of those deliciously dangerous drinks that will last you the whole evening.

Autumn Leaf

Autumn (or Fall as it's called there) is probably the prettiest time of year in North America. This little drink is the perfect way to toast the season's natural beauty. It doesn't matter too much if the colours blend…

ONE PART GREEN CRÈME DE MENTHE

ONE PART GALLIANO

ONE PART BRANDY

GRATED NUTMEG

❍ As with other shooters, use a small cylindrical glass and start by pouring in the crème de menthe.

❍ Now trickle the yellow Galliano carefully on the surface of the green and end by sliding a layer of golden brandy on top.

❍ Finish it off with a pinch of nutmeg.

Above: The Autumn Leaf is an attractive little shooter to drink when welcoming in the season of 'mists and mellow fruitfulness'.

Hudson Bay

The tough pioneers who explored Canada for the Hudson Bay Company certainly didn't hold back when it came to liquor. Who else would combine gin, brandy and rum in one drink?

ICE CUBES

TWO PARTS GIN

ONE PART CHERRY BRANDY

HALF A PART OF STRONG, DARK RUM

ONE PART ORANGE JUICE

JUICE OF HALF A LIME

SLICE OF LIME

○ Place four or five ice cubes in a cocktail shaker and add all the liquid ingredients.

○ Shake well and strain into a chilled cocktail glass.

○ Garnish with the slice of lime and serve.

Right: Assertive and strong, the Hudson Bay embodies the pioneering spirit of early Canadian explorers.

Above: The Canada Club adds a whole new dimension to Canadian whisky.

Canada Club

Like many countries, Canada produces whisky with a distinctive national character. Purists argue about whether the correct spelling of the Canadian product is with an 'e' or not. However you spell it, it's a proud national drink.

ICE CUBES
ONE PART CANADIAN WHISKY
THREE DASHES OF GRENADINE SYRUP
TWO DASHES OF ANGOSTURA BITTERS
LEMON PEEL
COCKTAIL CHERRY

○ Place four or five ice cubes in a bar glass and stir in the whisky, grenadine and Angostura bitters.

○ Strain into a cocktail glass and squeeze the lemon peel over it to add the zesty aroma.

○ Garnish with a cherry and serve.

Right: Although probably first made with Canadian whisky, Three Rivers tastes just as good made with any good whisky.

Three Rivers

Invented in Canada and often known by its French name, Trois Rivieres, this drink has become an international classic.

ICE CUBES
TWO PARTS WHISKY (PREFERABLY CANADIAN)
ONE PART DUBONNET
ONE PART TRIPLE SEC

○ Place four or five ice cubes in a cocktail shaker and add the whisky, Dubonnet and Triple Sec.

○ Shake well and strain into a lowball glass.

○ Serve ungarnished.

latin america and the caribbean

It is interesting that, while there are many poor countries in Latin America and the Caribbean, the people of these areas have a real feeling of the joy of a life filled with music, song and interesting drinks. This is reflected in some of the cocktails that originate in the regions.

El Burro

This delightful drink should be drunk in moderation if you don't want to make an ass of yourself!

CRUSHED ICE

ONE PART KAHLUA

ONE AND A HALF PARTS DARK RUM

ONE AND A HALF PARTS COCONUT CREAM

TWO PARTS THIN CREAM

HALF A BANANA

SPRIG OF FRESH MINT

SLICES OF BANANA

Above: The Chihuahua Bite is an aptly named, fierce little drink.

- ○ Place two spoonfuls of crushed ice in a blender and add all the other ingredients, except the mint and the slices of banana.
- ○ Blend at high speed for about 10 seconds.
- ○ Strain into a large goblet and garnish with the slices of banana and sprig of mint.

The Chihuahua Bite

Like the famous miniature Mexican dog, this drink may be petite but it certainly is lively.

ICE CUBES

THREE PARTS LONDON DRY GIN

ONE PART CALVADOS

ONE PART LIME JUICE CORDIAL

A TWIST OF LEMON RIND

- ○ Place three ice cubes in a cocktail shaker and add the gin, Calvados and lime juice cordial.
- ○ Shake well and strain into a cocktail glass.
- ○ Twist the lemon rind over it and drop it into the glass as garnish.

Opposite: El Burro is heavily loaded with all sorts of flavours and probably gets its name (the donkey) from the fact that it has quite a kick to it.

Tequila sunrise

TEQUILA, OF COURSE, is the national drink of Mexico, and this cocktail is one of many

based on the fiery spirit. It has become a cocktail classic.

ONE PART TEQUILA

THREE PARTS FRESH ORANGE JUICE

TWO DASHES OF GRENADINE

A MARASCHINO CHERRY

○ Pour the tequila and orange juice into a highball glass and stir them well.

○ Splash the grenadine on top of the mixture, close to the side of the glass, and watch the colour sink gently through the drink.

○ Garnish with a cherry on a cocktail stick.

Opposite: The Tequila Sunrise gets its name from its stunning appearance. Tequila is a spirit distilled from the agave cactus and forms the basis of many well-known cocktails.

Above: The Mexican Ruin is good with coffee, or even instead of coffee.

Mexican Ruin

Tequila has probably been the ruin of many a Mexican, but this elegant variation should not leave too wide a trail of destruction in its wake.

CRUSHED ICE

ONE PART TEQUILA

ONE PART COFFEE LIQUEUR

○ Place a scoop of crushed ice in a cocktail mixing glass.

○ Add the tequila and coffee liqueur and stir well.

○ Strain into a cocktail glass and serve.

Montezuma

Mexico again, and this time it's a really unusual drink that looks good and tastes wonderful.

CRUSHED ICE (OR ICE CUBES IF USING A SHAKER)

ONE EGG YOLK

TWO PARTS TEQUILA

ONE PART MADEIRA WINE

○ Place a scoop of crushed ice in a blender (or four ice cubes in a cocktail shaker) and add the egg yolk, tequila and Madeira wine.

○ Blend for about 15 seconds, or shake very vigorously, and strain the drink into a chilled cocktail glass.

TNT (Tequila 'n' Tonic)

Anything based on tequila is likely to produce interesting results. This one's not a drink for the faint-hearted.

ICE CUBES

TWO PARTS TEQUILA

HALF A PART FRESH LIME JUICE

TONIC WATER

LEMON PEEL

○ Place three ice cubes in a bar glass, add the tequila and lime juice and stir well.

○ Strain into a lowball glass, top up with tonic water and garnish with a twist of lemon peel.

Below left: The TNT, a drink with a potentially explosive result; *Below right:* The Montezuma, in which egg yolk is used to create the golden hue.

margarita

NOBODY REMEMBERS who Margarita was, but her name lives on in this fiery little drink, which can be served straight up or frozen.

CRUSHED ICE

THREE PARTS TEQUILA

ONE PART TRIPLE SEC

ONE PART LIME JUICE (PREFERABLY FRESH)

ONE EGG WHITE OR LEMON JUICE

SALT

ICE CUBES

○ Place a scoop of crushed ice in a blender or shaker and add the tequila, Triple Sec and lime juice. Blend or shake well.

○ Dip the rim of a cocktail glass in egg white or lemon juice and frost with salt.

○ Add two ice cubes and gently pour the Margarita mixture over them, taking care not to disturb the salt frosting.

Opposite: The Margarita, probably the best known of all tequila-based drinks, is traditionally served in a salt-rimmed cocktail glass.

The Sombrero

Here's a cheerful little splash of Mexican magic to get you throwing your hat in the air.

ONE PART KAHLUA

ONE PART THICK CREAM

○ Chill the Kahlua well and pour it into a shot glass.

○ Trickle the cream onto the Kahlua, letting it run over the back of a spoon.

○ Serve with a steady hand.

Above: It takes a steady hand to form a clean dividing line between the ingredients of the Sombrero.

Acapulco Joy

This classic cocktail is a fine after dinner warmer, with its rich, coffee flavour. It can also be served as a nice boozy dessert.

THREE PARTS KAHLUA

TWO PARTS PEACH SCHNAPPS

ONE SCOOP VANILLA ICE CREAM

HALF A RIPE BANANA, SLICED

A PINCH OF GROUND NUTMEG

A MARASCHINO CHERRY

○ Place the Kahlua, schnapps, ice cream and banana in a blender and blend until smooth and creamy.

○ Pour into a chilled wine goblet, sprinkle with the pinch of nutmeg and add the cherry as garnish.

Above: The Acapulco Joy is the perfect end to a good meal, whether eaten or drunk.

Pancho Villa

This very lively drink was designed to commemorate the spirit of the rebel general of the Mexican Revolution, who invaded American territory and led the US Army on a chase for many months.

CRUSHED ICE

ONE PART LIGHT RUM

ONE PART GIN

ONE PART APRICOT BRANDY

ONE PART PINEAPPLE JUICE

A DASH OF CHERRY BRANDY

○ Place a scoop of crushed ice in a cocktail shaker, add all the ingredients and shake well.

○ Strain into a chilled cocktail glass – or wine goblet – and serve.

Right: A powerful drink in memory of a strong man who dared to challenge the American army.

Xalapa Punch

This cocktail probably originated from Xalapa, a cathedral town situated in the province of Vera Cruz in Mexico.

Here again, the size of your measure will be determined by the size of your punch bowl. In these informal times almost any large bowl will do. I have even seen punch served in a brass-bound wooden bucket. It looked great!

THE ZEST OF TWO LARGE ORANGES, GRATED

TWO PARTS STRONG BLACK TEA

HONEY OR SUGAR TO TASTE (ABOUT A CUPFUL)

ONE PART GOLDEN RUM

ONE PART CALVADOS

ONE PART RED WINE

A BLOCK OF ICE

ORANGE AND LEMON SLICES

○ Place the grated orange zest in a saucepan and pour the hot tea over it to absorb the flavour. Leave it to cool and add the honey or sugar. Stir until dissolved.

○ Add the rum, Calvados and red wine and place in the fridge to chill.

○ When ready to serve, place the block of ice in the punch bowl, pour the punch over it and garnish it with slices of orange and lemon.

Above: El Diablo – a devishly tempting drink, as its name implies.

El Diablo

Although it is called 'The Devil', this South American drink is cool and refreshing.

ICE CUBES

THREE PARTS TEQUILA

THREE PARTS FRESH LIME JUICE

ONE PART CRÈME DE CASSIS

TWO PARTS GINGER ALE

○ Fill a highball glass with ice cubes.

○ Add the tequila, lime juice and crème de cassis and stir well.

○ Add the ginger ale and stir again lightly before serving.

The Aztec

This drink was certainly not part of the ancient Aztec culture, but was invented in Arizona, USA, to pay tribute to a once-great civilization.

CRUSHED ICE

TWO PARTS GIN

ONE PART CHERRY BRANDY

TWO PARTS PIÑA COLADA

TWO PARTS ORANGE JUICE

A SLICE OF PINEAPPLE

A MARASCHINO CHERRY

○ Place a scoop of crushed ice in a shaker and add the gin, cherry brandy, Piña Colada and orange juice.

○ Shake well and strain into a tall glass.

○ Garnish with the pineapple slice and cherry.

Right: All the flavours of a tropical fruit salad are in the Aztec, a tall and delightful drink.

Picador

Several South American countries have a bull-fighting tradition inherited from their Spanish colonists. This one, named after the picador, brings you the excitement of the bullring without the cruelty.

ICE CUBES

ONE PART TEQUILA

ONE PART KAHLUA

A TWIST OF LEMON PEEL

○ Place four or five ice cubes in a cocktail shaker and add the tequila and Kahlua in equal, but generous parts.

○ Shake well and strain into a cocktail glass.

○ Garnish with a twist of lemon peel and serve.

Left: The Picador offers the excitement of the bullring, but without the dust and blood.

The Frozen Matador

Bullfighting usually takes place in the heat and dust of summer, so there is something rare and unusual about a frozen matador, just as there is about this very refreshing cocktail.

CRUSHED ICE

ONE PART TEQUILA

ONE PART FRESH PINEAPPLE JUICE

A DASH OF FRESH LIME JUICE

ICE CUBES

SLICES OF PINEAPPLE

MINT LEAVES

○ For this drink a blender is essential. Place two generous scoops of crushed ice in the blender and add the tequila, pineapple juice and lime juice. Blend to a frothy mixture.

○ Strain into a lowball glass, add two ice cubes and garnish with the pineapple slices and the mint leaves.

Above: After the excitement of the bullring, the Frozen Matador offers a cool, refreshing break.

Piñata

The piñata is traditionally a papier-mâché container filled with small gifts and hung from a tree bough, to be beaten open with sticks at festival times. This piñata is just as rewarding and has a real South American flavour.

ICE CUBES

ONE PART TEQUILA

ONE PART BANANA LIQUEUR

ONE PART FRESH LIME JUICE

○ Place five or six ice cubes in a cocktail shaker.

○ Add the tequila, banana liqueur and lime juice and shake well.

○ Fill a lowball glass or large wine goblet with ice cubes and strain the cocktail mixture over them.

○ Serve ungarnished.

Right: No Mexican party is complete without the fun of a piñana, whether it's the baubles or the drink.

Santa Fe Prickly Margarita

The prickly pear, with its broad leaves and spiky fruit, is indigenous to most South American countries. The juice of the fruit is deliciously sweet and a natural cocktail ingredient.

FOUR PARTS TEQUILA

ONE PART FRESH LIME JUICE

ONE PART FRESH GRAPEFRUIT JUICE

TWO PARTS PRICKLY PEAR JUICE

ONE PART ORANGE JUICE

ONE PART COINTREAU

ICE CUBES

FINE TABLE SALT

TWIST OF LEMON RIND

○ Shake all the liquid ingredients with five or six ice cubes in a cocktail shaker.

○ Frost the rim of a cocktail glass with the salt and carefully fill the glass with the cocktail mix, taking care not to disturb the salt.

○ Garnish with a twist of lemon rind and serve.

Left: Prickly pear juice may not be in everybody's fridge, but if you can find it, this is the way to enjoy it most.

Mañana

Tomorrow – *mañana* – is always a good time in the summer heat of South American countries. Today is far too hot to do very much, except maybe drink a refreshing rum cocktail.

ICE CUBES

ONE PART APRICOT BRANDY

FOUR PARTS LIGHT RUM

A SPLASH OF LEMON JUICE

CRUSHED ICE

○ Place four or five ice cubes in a cocktail shaker and add the brandy, rum and lemon juice.

○ Shake well and pour over crushed ice in a lowball glass.

○ Serve ungarnished

Above: You don't have to wait until tomorrow to enjoy today's mañana.

Punta del Este

Punta del Este is an elegant seaside resort on the mouth of the Rio de la Plata in Uruguay. At almost any time of day you can see wealthy motor yacht owners sipping cocktails on the decks of their elegant craft. This one was probably invented there.

CRUSHED ICE

THREE PARTS LIGHT RUM

ONE PART CRÈME DE CACAO

ONE PART COCONUT RUM, SUCH AS MALIBU

THREE PARTS PINEAPPLE JUICE

ONE PART FRESH CREAM

ONE PART CRANBERRY JUICE

○ Place a scoop of crushed ice in a cocktail shaker and add all the ingredients.

○ Shake well and strain into a highball glass

○ Serve ungarnished, or with extra ice if required.

Right: Rum, pineapple and coconut help to create this creamy South American drink.

Pineapple Francine

Although pineapples in various forms are now available worldwide, they originated in South America, where rum is also a favourite spirit.

This delicious tropical fruit-salad flavoured cocktail is best enjoyed while relaxing on a warm summer's day.

CRUSHED ICE

ONE PART LIGHT RUM

ONE PART APRICOT BRANDY OR LIQUEUR

TWP PARTS PINEAPPLE JUICE

TWO PARTS FRESH CREAM

TWO PARTS CRUSHED PINEAPPLE CHUNKS (BLENDED INTO

A SMOOTH PUREE)

- ❍ Place about a cup of crushed ice in a cocktail shaker and add the rum, apricot liqueur, pineapple juice, cream and pineapple puree.
- ❍ Shake well and strain into a large wine goblet.
- ❍ Serve ungarnished.

Above: This rich, creamy drink is an ideal summer simmer for tropical nights. It could even double as a dessert.

Pineapple Bomber

This is another popular rum-based drink, with the pineapple flavour of the Caribbean.

ONE PART AMARETTO

TWO PARTS DARK RUM

TWO PARTS SOUTHERN COMFORT

SIX PARTS PINEAPPLE JUICE

ICE CUBES

○ Add the Amaretto, rum, Southern Comfort and pineapple juice to a cocktail shaker and shake vigorously.

○ Fill a highball glass with ice cubes and pour the shaken cocktail mix over them.

○ Serve ungarnished.

Pineapple Gimlet

This is a tropical version of the popular Gimlet cocktail and it incorporates the tangy fruitiness of a ripe pineapple.

The Pineapple Gimlet is such a popular drink that it is a good idea to mix the ingredients in a large jug and pour over ice as required.

ICE CUBES

THREE PARTS LONDON DRY GIN

ONE PART FRESHLY SQUEEZED LIME JUICE

SIX PARTS PINEAPPLE JUICE

○ Fill a highball glass with ice cubes and pour the ingredients over them.

○ Stir well and serve ungarnished.

Pirates of the Caribbean

This cocktail is a recent invention, inspired by the series of films of the same name, so it probably owes it existence more to Disneyland than the real Caribbean.

CRUSHED ICE

TWO PARTS GOLD PUERTO RICAN RUM

ONE PART DARK JAMAICAN RUM

THREE PARTS CRANBERRY JUICE

ONE PART LIME JUICE

CASTER SUGAR TO TASTE

ONE EGG WHITE

○ Place a scoop of crushed ice in a shaker or electric blender and add all the ingredients.

○ Shake well, or blend until smooth, and pour into a chilled lowball glass.

○ Serve ungarnished.

Opposite top: The Pineapple Bomber is a dark and warming drink.

Opposite below: In contrast, the Pineapple Gimlet is a cool, crisp summer drink that can be served long or short.

Right: Pirates would have loved this delightful drink as a change from their rum ration.

The Zombie

A zombie is a corpse that has been brought
back to life. Maybe the name of this cocktail
refers to its restorative powers.

ICE CUBES

ONE PART DARK RUM

ONE PART LIGHT RUM

ONE PART APRICOT BRANDY

ONE PART FRESH PINEAPPLE JUICE

A SQUEEZE OF LEMON JUICE

A SQUEEZE OF ORANGE JUICE

A SLICE OF PINEAPPLE

○ Place four ice cubes in a cocktail shaker and
add the dark and light rum, brandy, pineapple
juice and the two squeezes of citrus juice.

○ Shake well and strain into a wine goblet.

○ Garnish with a slice of pineapple and a cherry
threaded together on a cocktail stick.

Zombie Punch

There is something a little mysterious about the idea of a zombie, and this drink certainly has a murky and mysterious look to match its name. The flavour, however, is full of life.

TWO PARTS LIGHT PUERTO RICAN RUM

ONE PART DARK JAMAICAN RUM

ONE PART DARK DEMERARA RUM

ONE PART TRIPLE SEC

ONE PART FRESH LIME JUICE

ONE PART FRESH ORANGE JUICE

A QUARTER PART LEMON JUICE

A QUARTER PART PAPAYA JUICE

A QUARTER PART PINEAPPLE JUICE

A SPLASH OF PERNOD

A LARGE CHUNK OF ICE

PINEAPPLE SLICES

○ Mix all the liquid ingredients together in a large punch bowl, place the ice in the centre and allow it to stand for a few hours to chill.

○ Before the guests arrive, taste it and adjust the flavour by adding the appropriate fruit juices or spirits.

○ Garnish with slices of pineapple and serve.

Opposite: The Zombie is lively enough to wake the deadest party.

Left: Like all punches, the Zombie Punch is a crowd pleaser that can be made well in advance of the first guests' arrival.

mojito

THIS CLASSIC COCKTAIL is probably known in every cocktail bar in the world. Like all classics, it blends sweet with sour to perfection.

JUICE OF HALF A LIME
WHITE SUGAR TO TASTE
SPRIGS OF MINT
CRUSHED ICE
TWO PARTS LIGHT RUM
CLUB SODA (OPTIONAL)

○ Squeeze the lime into a chilled lowball glass, add the sugar and mint and muddle with a bar spoon until the sugar has dissolved and the mint leaves are well crushed.

○ Now fill the glass with crushed ice and swizzle until the ingredients are nicely mixed.

○ Pour in the rum and stir. At this stage you may wish to add chilled club soda to fill the glass before serving.

Opposite: By adjusting the proportion of soda, the Mojito can be made as strong – or as weak – as you like.

Above: The Rum Drop-shot has layer upon layer of flavour.

Rum Drop-shot

Ideally a strong demerara rum should be used in this drink, but any boldly flavoured rum will do.

CRUSHED ICE

FOUR PARTS STRONG DARK RUM

ONE PART COCONUT CREAM

ONE PART LEMON JUICE

PINEAPPLE PIECE

○ Place a scoop of crushed ice in a shaker or blender, add the rum, coconut cream and lemon juice and shake or blend until smooth.

○ Strain into a cocktail glass and serve, decorated with a pineapple piece on a cocktail stick.

Caribbean Champagne Cocktail

This recipe reminds us of palm-fringed sandy beaches and thatched umbrellas that keep the sun's harsh rays from warming our chilled glasses.

ONE PART LIGHT RUM

ONE PART BANANA LIQUEUR

A DASH OF ANGOSTURA BITTERS

FIVE PARTS CHILLED CHAMPAGNE

A SLICE OF BANANA, CUT LENGTHWISE

○ Pour the rum, banana liqueur and Angostura bitters into a chilled Champagne flute and stir well.

○ Add the chilled champagne to fill the glass and slip in the long slice of banana as garnish before serving.

Above: Champagne adds a cool sophistication to any cocktail.

cuba libre

THIS CUBAN CLASSIC is reputed to have been invented by an army officer shortly after Coca-Cola was first produced back in the 1890s.

CRUSHED ICE
ONE GENEROUS PART LIGHT RUM
THE JUICE OF A LIME
COLA
A SLICE OF LIME

○ In a highball glass, place a small scoop of crushed ice and pour in the rum and lime juice.

○ Top up with cola and garnish with a thin wedge of fresh lime.

○ It is usually served with a swizzle stick or stirrer.

Opposite: The old song comes to life in this rum and cola classic.

Above: A Caribbean version of the famous Irish Coffee.

Jamaican Coffee

Whenever a good drink is invented, it's not long before it is copied and adapted around the world. This is a tropical version of the ever-popular Irish Coffee.

ONE PART TIA MARIA

ONE PART JAMAICAN RUM

FRESHLY MADE HOT BLACK COFFEE

WHIPPED CREAM

○ Pour the Tia Maria and rum into a tall coffee mug – a glass Irish coffee mug is ideal – and fill the mug almost to the brim with coffee.

○ Float a generous blob of whipped cream on the top and serve.

The Tall Islander

The name refers to the length of the drink, rather than its creator. It's long and cooling and has a distinctly tropical flavour, ideal for sipping on a deserted beach.

ICE CUBES

ONE PART LIGHT RUM

A DASH OF DARK JAMAICAN RUM

ONE PART PINEAPPLE JUICE

A DASH OF LIME JUICE

ONE TEASPOON OF SUGAR SYRUP

CHILLED SODA WATER

A SLICE OF LIME

○ Place four ice cubes in a cocktail shaker and add the light and dark rum, pineapple juice, lime juice and sugar syrup.

○ Shake well and strain into a highball glass.

○ Add a splash of soda water and several ice cubes.

○ Garnish with the slice of lime.

Opposite bottom: Cuban rum and pineapple form a natural combination in this tangy tropical drink.

Havana Beach

Cuba is known for more than just cigars; some excellent rum is made there, too! This tangy drink makes full use of the island's flavours.

CRUSHED ICE

ONE PART LIGHT CUBAN RUM

ONE PART PINEAPPLE JUICE

ONE QUARTER FRESH LIME, CUT INTO PIECES

GINGER ALE

○ Place a scoop of crushed ice in a blender and add the rum, pineapple juice and lime pieces.

○ Blend for quite a while, until it is smooth and frothy.

○ Pour it into a highball glass and top up with ginger ale. Garnish with a twist of the lime rind.

Above: Boca Chica – is it a drink or a pudding? You decide.

Boca Chica Coffee

The use of coffee and ice cream in cocktails is not unusual, and the good thing is that these recipes need just a little adjustment to turn them into delicious puddings. Quantities can be varied to taste.

ONE SCOOP VANILLA ICE CREAM

ONE GENEROUS PART OF DARK JAMAICA RUM

COLD STRONG BLACK COFFEE AS REQUIRED

○ Stir the rum and ice cream together in a lowball glass until it is smooth but not completely liquid.

○ Top up with coffee, stir gently and serve.

Daiquiri

MAN IS A CREATIVE ANIMAL and has been shown to adapt to almost any circumstances.

American engineers working in Daiquiri, Cuba, were upset to discover they could not

obtain their usual drink, bourbon, there. But there was rum in plentiful supply, so they

set about creating a drink to replace their favourite tipple. The daiquiri was born.

ICE CUBES

ONE PART LIGHT RUM (TRADITIONALLY CUBAN, OF COURSE)

THE JUICE OF HALF A LIME

HALF A TEASPOON OF SUGAR

A SLICE OF LIME

A COCKTAIL CHERRY

○ Place four or five ice cubes in a cocktail shaker. Add the rum, lime juice and sugar.

○ Shake very thoroughly, then strain into a cocktail glass.

○ Decorate with a slice of lime and the cocktail cherry spiked on a stick.

Opposite: Ernest Hemingway always ordered double Daiquiris when he frequented La Floradita Bar in Havana, Cuba.

Banana Daiquiri

In his popular Discworld novels, author Terry Pratchett writes about an orang-utan who is inordinately fond of banana daiquiris. Readers all over the world send Pratchett recipes for this now-famous drink. This one is from a South African fan, although it has the flavour of the Caribbean.

TWO PARTS LIGHT RUM

ONE PART BANANA LIQUEUR

ONE PART FRESH LIME JUICE

HALF A MEDIUM-SIZED BANANA

CRUSHED ICE

A SLICE OF KIWI FRUIT, IF AVAILABLE

○ Place the rum, liqueur, lime juice and banana in a blender and blend for about ten seconds until smooth and creamy.

○ Add two generous scoops of crushed ice and blend for a further second or two, just to chill the drink.

○ Strain the mixture into a goblet, garnish with the slice of kiwi fruit (or you could use a slice of banana in an emergency) and serve with a straw.

Daiquiri Blossom

Not everybody enjoys the sharp astringency of the daiquiri described in the previous recipe. Maybe it was fine for homesick mining engineers, but in the comfort of your own home or a cosy cocktail bar you may prefer this sweeter version. It certainly has a tropical flavour to it.

ICE CUBES

ONE PART LIGHT RUM

ONE PART FRESHLY SQUEEZED ORANGE JUICE

A DASH OF MARASCHINO

A SLICE OF ORANGE

A COCKTAIL CHERRY

○ Place four or five ice cubes in a cocktail shaker. Add the rum, orange juice and maraschino.

○ Shake well and strain into a cocktail glass.

○ Decorate with the slice of orange and the cherry speared together on a cocktail stick.

Above from left to right: Banana Daiquiri, Daiquiri Blossom and Frozen Pineapple Daiquiri – the Daiquiri comes in many guises.

Frozen Pineapple Daiquiri

Of course, you can go all the way with the tropical drink theme and make this rather exotic version of the famous drink. Looks good, tastes great!

ONE PART LIGHT RUM (NATURALLY)

JUICE OF HALF A LIME

TWO TEASPOONS OF COINTREAU

TWO SLICES OF RIPE PINEAPPLE, CUT INTO CUBES

CRUSHED ICE

A COCKTAIL CHERRY

○ Place the rum, lime juice, Cointreau and pineapple cubes in a blender and give them a whizz until the mixture is smooth and frothy.

○ Half fill a champagne flute with crushed ice and pour the mixture over it.

○ Decorate with a final cube of pineapple and the cherry spiked together on a cocktail stick.

europe

After many centuries of wine and brandy-based entertaining, Europe was lured into the exciting world of cocktails in the 20th century, when American writers and artists made cities like Paris and Rome their new gathering places. Today the cocktail rules supreme in many sophsticated European bars.

The International

One of the reasons this cocktail got its name is that it combines the flavours typical of several national drinks: vodka from Russia, cognac and Cointreau from France and ouzo from Greece.

CRUSHED ICE

TWO PARTS COGNAC

HALF A PART VODKA

HALF A PART OUZO

HALF A PART COINTREAU

◯ Place two scoops of crushed ice in a bar mixing glass and add the cognac, vodka, ouzo and Cointreau.

◯ Stir well and strain into a chilled cocktail glass.

◯ Serve ungarnished, or decorate with a tiny flag.

Left: The spirit of European unity is captured perfectly in this combination of national drinks.

Above: The Cardinale is another of Harry's famous, gin-based cocktails and could be called a martini with a difference.

Pink Gin

While we are on the subject of pretty colours for drinks, let's take a look at that very English drink, Pink Gin. The famous round-the-world sailor Sir Francis Chichester claims that it was Pink Gins that kept him cheerful (dare we say in good spirits) during his epic voyage.

The British do it the simple way. They just shake a couple of dashes of Angostura bitters into a glass, swirl it about to coat the inside and then add a dollop of gin.

Americans tend to prefer a slightly more precise version.

ICE CUBES

TWO DASHES OF ANGOSTURA BITTERS

TWO MEASURES OF DRY GIN

A TWIST OF LEMON PEEL (OPTIONAL)

- Place four ice cubes in a bar glass and add the bitters.
- Pour in the gin and stir well. Strain into a chilled cocktail glass.
- Usually served ungarnished, but you could add a twist of lemon peel for decoration.

Cardinale

This cocktail has become so popular that it is available in bottled form, ready-mixed, all over Europe and America.

SIX PARTS GIN

ONE PART DRY VERMOUTH

THREE PARTS CAMPARI

ICE CUBES

- In a bar glass, stir together the gin, vermouth and Campari with three ice cubes.
- Strain into a cocktail glass and serve.

Above: Rolls Royce, a cocktail as elegant as the car it is named after.

Above: The Salty Dog is to vodka what margarita is to tequila.

The Rolls Royce

Perhaps this drink was designed to be served in the back of a Rolls as the chauffeur drives you silently through the British countryside.

CRUSHED ICE

ONE PART COGNAC

ONE PART COINTREAU

ONE PART ORANGE JUICE

○ Place three scoops of crushed ice in a cocktail shaker and add the cognac, Cointreau and orange juice.

○ Shake well, then strain the contents into a chilled cocktail glass.

○ Serve ungarnished.

Salty Dog

This is the ideal drink to sip during Cowes' Week, an annual regatta held at the Isle of Wight, off the southern coast of England. Old sea dogs gather to watch the young skippers.

ICE CUBES

FOUR PARTS VODKA

ONE PART UNSWEETENED GRAPEFRUIT JUICE

ONE TEASPOON LEMON JUICE

SALT

○ Place three ice cubes in a cocktail shaker and add the vodka, grapefruit juice and lemon juice and shake well.

○ Frost the rim of a chilled cocktail glass with fine salt and strain the cocktail into the glass.

Old Oxford University Punch

Most of the Oxford academic year is in winter when the air is chilly in the draughty old college buildings. No doubt many a long and otherwise boring tutorial has been made more bearable by a warming mug of punch.

ONE CUP OF BROWN SUGAR

BOILING WATER

THREE CUPS OF LEMON JUICE

ONE BOTTLE OF COGNAC

CINNAMON STICKS AND WHOLE CLOVES

ONE BOTTLE OF DARK DEMERARA RUM

○ Dissolve the sugar in the boiling water in a saucepan on low heat on the stove. Keep it hot, but ensure it does not boil at any stage. Add the lemon juice, cognac, cinnamon sticks and cloves when the sugar has dissolved.

○ Pour in almost all the rum, leaving about half a cup in the bottle.

○ Shortly before serving, place the remaining rum in a ladle and heat over a flame. Light the rum in the ladle, pour the flaming spirit onto the surface of the punch and serve. If the flames are still flickering, extinguish them with the lid of the saucepan.

Above: Old Oxford University Punch was designed to keep out the chill.

Tom collins

MANY PEOPLE refer to this drink as a 'John Collins' and this is understandable. The original Collins was indeed a John, the head waiter at Limmer's Hotel in London in the 18th century. He is reputed to have used the rather heavy and oily Dutch-style gin in his drink, which was not very popular in America. One barman decided to use a London brand of gin called Old Tom in the cocktail instead. The drink gained popularity instantly and became known as the Tom Collins.

ONE PART DRY GIN
ONE OR TWO DASHES OF SUGAR SYRUP
THE JUICE OF ONE LEMON
SODA WATER
ICE CUBES
A SLICE OF LEMON

○ Pour the gin, sugar syrup and lemon juice into a highball glass and stir it with a swizzle stick.
○ Top up the glass with chilled soda water, add an ice cube if required and garnish with a slice of lemon.

Opposite: The Tom Collins was originally made with heavy Dutch gin. Today, the lighter style of London gin is preferred.

Grog

Named after 'Old Grog', a Royal Navy captain who dressed in a coat made of grogram material, this warming drink was served as a daily ration to sailors. It was usually made in bulk and issued from a large grog can, but we prefer a smaller, more refined helping.

A SLICE OF LEMON

FOUR WHOLE CLOVES

A CUBE OF SUGAR

TWO PARTS BOILING WATER

ONE PART DARK JAMAICAN RUM

HALF A CINNAMON STICK

○ Stud the lemon slice with the cloves and place it in a warmed mug with the sugar cube.

○ Pour on the boiling water to dissolve the sugar

○ Add the rum, stir with the cinnamon stick and serve in the same mug.

Right: Henry Morgan's Grog is a pirate version of grog, the Royal Navy's drink comprising equal quantities of rum and water.

Henry Morgan's Grog

Captain Morgan's version of grog is rather different and far more powerful than the grog served to sailors.

CRUSHED ICE

ONE PART DARK JAMAICAN RUM

TWO PARTS PERNOD

TWO PARTS WHISKY

ONE PART THICK CREAM

GROUND NUTMEG

○ Place a scoop of crushed ice in a blender or cocktail shaker and add the rum, Pernod, whisky and cream.

○ Blend or shake briskly until well mixed, and then strain into a lowball glass.

○ Dust with ground nutmeg before serving.

Hot Buttered Rum

No collection of rum drinks would be complete without at least one recipe for hot buttered rum. It's a warm, sustaining drink to serve on a freezing winter's night by a roaring log fire. Buttered rum is mentioned by Charles Dickens in his book *Hard Times*. 'Take a glass of scalding rum and butter before you get into bed,' Bounderby says to Mrs Sparsit.

THE PEEL OF A LEMON OR ORANGE

WHOLE CLOVES

ONE TABLESPOON OF BROWN SUGAR

A CINNAMON STICK

A LIBERAL HELPING OF DARK JAMAICAN RUM

HALF AS MUCH CRÈME DE CACAO

A PAT OF UNSALTED BUTTER

GRATED NUTMEG

○ Warm a large coffee mug by filling it with boiling water and letting it stand for a minute. While it is warming, take the citrus peel and stud it with as many whole cloves as you can.

○ Empty the coffee mug and place the studded peel in it, together with the brown sugar and cinnamon stick. Add a little boiling water and stir until the sugar has dissolved.

○ Now add the rum and crème de cacao and fill the mug with hot water.

○ Remove the cinnamon stick. Drop in the butter, stir and sprinkle with grated nutmeg.

Right: In parts of Britian and America Hot Buttered Rum is as popular as Glühwein or the Tom and Jerry as a winter tradition.

Brass Monkey

The 'brass monkey' is essentially a Royal Navy expression. It was the name given to the brass rack on which cannon balls were stored in the days of sailing ship warfare.

In very cold weather the brass would contract and sometimes the cannon balls would no longer fit on the shrunken monkey and would pop out, causing some confusion as they rolled about on the gun deck.

Hence the expression: 'Cold enough to freeze the balls off a brass monkey.'

The cocktail is a good warmer when the temperature reaches brass monkey levels.

ICE CUBES

ONE PART LIGHT RUM

ONE PART VODKA

FOUR PARTS ORANGE JUICE

A SLICE OF ORANGE

○ Fill a highball glass with ice cubes and pour the rum, vodka and orange juice over them.

○ Stir carefully and serve decorated with the slice of orange and a pretty straw.

Right: The Brass Monkey has nothing to do with primates but originated, not surprisingly, in the navy.

Lady Hunt

An elegant and delicious cocktail that is tangy and crisp in character, but also gently mellow. The original version of the Lady Hunt was created by Salvatore Calabrese, one of Britain's best-known bartenders, specially for Lady Caroline Hunt, the founder of Rosewood Hotels.

THREE PARTS MALT WHISKY

ONE PART TIA MARIA

ONE PART AMARETTO

THE JUICE OF HALF A LEMON

A DASH OF EGG WHITE

ICE CUBES

A SLICE OF ORANGE

A MARASCHINO CHERRY

Above: The elegant Lady Hunt cocktail.

○ Place all the ingredients with the exception of the orange slice and cherry into a cocktail shaker with four ice cubes and shake briskly.

○ Strain into a cocktail glass and decorate with the slice of orange and the maraschino cherry.

Above: Another vodka-based cocktail, the Q Martini has the added attraction of being blue.

Vodkatini

It's interesting to see what factors influence the popularity of a cocktail. The vodka martini must be one of the best-known cocktails in the world today, just because the famous and fictitious James Bond, 007, has been drinking vodka martinis for the past 36 years. The perfect example of suave British understatement.

ICE CUBES

TWO PARTS VODKA (PREFERABLY FROM RUSSIA)

ONE PART DRY VERMOUTH

A TWIST OF LEMON RIND

○ Place about five ice cubes in a bar glass, add the vodka and vermouth and stir well.

○ Strain the mixture into a cocktail glass and decorate it with a twist of lemon rind.

The Q Martini

The James Bond series of books and films has spawned a number of popular drinks, including this intriguing blue version of the Martini.

ICE CUBES

TWO PARTS VODKA

A SPLASH OF BLUE CURAÇAO

HALF A PART LIME JUICE

A TWIST OF LEMON RIND

○ Place three ice cubes in a cocktail bar glass. Add the vodka, blue Curaçao and lime juice.

○ Stir until well blended and strain into a cocktail glass.

○ Decorate with a twist of lemon rind.

Sherry Shandy

Although port and lemon was considered the traditional London prostitutes' drink, sherry retained its respectability and many a young debutante was introduced to the delights of the cocktail circuit with this gentle drink, which can be made as strong or weak as you please.

THREE DASHES OF ANGOSTURA BITTERS

TWO SHERRY GLASSES OF AMONTILLADO SHERRY

A BOTTLE OF GINGER ALE OR GINGER BEER

ICE CUBES

A SLICE OF LEMON

◯ Splash the bitters into a chilled highball glass and swirl it around to coat the inside of the glass.

◯ Pour in the sherry and fill the glass with the ginger ale or ginger beer.

◯ Float an ice cube on the top and serve garnished with a slice of lemon.

The Bee's Kiss

Bees and blossoms kiss in the warmth of an English summer garden. A touch of rich Devonshire cream adds smooth delight to this sweet drink.

CRUSHED ICE

TWO PARTS LIGHT RUM

ONE PART CLEAR HONEY

ONE PART THICK CREAM

◯ Place a cup of crushed ice in a cocktail shaker and pour over the rum, honey and cream.

◯ Shake vigorously until well blended.

◯ Strain into a chilled cocktail glass and serve ungarnished.

Right: The Bee's Kiss is one of remarkably few cocktails to specify honey as an ingredient.

Eggnog

Traditionally this was the drink served in English country homes on Christmas morning to keep out the chill. The eggnog probably derived its name from the term 'noggin', which was a small glass of strong beer. Some folk enjoyed this with an egg beaten in to thicken it. Nowadays, we prefer brandy and rum instead of beer. It's one of the few cocktails in this collection that does not involve ice.

ONE PART BRANDY

ONE PART DARK RUM

A FRESH EGG

A DASH OF SWEET SYRUP

FIVE PARTS FULL-CREAM MILK

WHOLE NUTMEG

○ Place the brandy, rum, egg and syrup in a shaker and shake vigorously to create a creamy consistency.

○ Strain it into a highball glass, add the milk and stir it gently.

○ Grate a sprinkling of nutmeg over it and serve at room temperature.

Left: Eggnog is a drink that will warm the chilliest of winter mornings – you may even use warm milk.

Sherry Eggnog

The Sherry Eggnog is a smooth and sensual drink with a velvety texture.

CRUSHED ICE

TWO SHERRY GLASSES OF AMONTILLADO SHERRY

A DESSERTSPOON OF CASTER SUGAR (OR TO TASTE)

A FRESH EGG

A CUP OF MILK

GRATED NUTMEG

○ Place half a cup of crushed ice in a blender or cocktail shaker. Add the sherry, caster sugar, egg and milk and shake or blend until smooth and velvety.

○ Strain into a chilled highball glass and dust with grated nutmeg.

Above: Quite apart from being a delicious, silky-smooth drink, the Sherry Eggnog is reputed to be soothing for a sore throat and helpful for a hangover.

Right: Mulled Claret is a more refined version of the traditional winter drink, originally made simply by heating a fire poker and plunging it into a tankard of wine.

Mulled Claret

Mulled wine has been a traditional winter drink in Britain for centuries. Modern recipes, compared with those of days gone by, are slightly more refined, better tasting and certainly with more of a kick.

THE PEEL OF A LEMON

SIX WHOLE CLOVES

GROUND CINNAMON TO TASTE

A PINCH OF GRATED NUTMEG

FIVE PARTS RED BORDEAUX-STYLE WINE

ONE PART RUBY PORT

ONE PART BRANDY

○ Place the lemon peel, cloves, cinnamon and nutmeg in a saucepan, add the liquid ingredients and heat slowly until almost, but not quite, boiling. If it is allowed to boil it loses its alcohol.

○ Strain the drink into a warmed coffee mug.

Rossini

Here's a pretty and refreshing drink to serve when strawberries are in season – perfect while watching tennis at Wimbledon.

ONE PART PURÉED STRAWBERRIES

THREE PARTS DRY SPARKLING WINE

ONE FRESH STRAWBERRY

○ Pour the strawberry purée into a champagne flute and top up with chilled sparkling wine. Stir very gently, trying not to dissipate the bubbles.

○ Float the fresh strawberry on top and serve.

Left: The Rossini, a variation of the Bellini, uses fresh strawberry purée instead of peach juice.

Left: Black Velvet is traditionally served in a beer tankard, but in modern, more refined times, a champagne flute is often used instead.

Black Velvet

It's not difficult to see how this old favourite got its name. A good stout has a smooth, creamy consistency rather like liquid velvet, and the sparkling wine adds a special glow.

A BOTTLE OR CAN OF GUINNESS STOUT

A BOTTLE OF DRY CHAMPAGNE

❍ Half-fill the glass with the stout, then gently pour in the champagne, trying to create as little foam as possible.

❍ Serve without ice or garnish.

Prince of Wales

This champagne-based drink has a royal connection. It was probably a favourite of Queen Victoria's son, Alfred, who seems to have led a merry life as he toured about the British Empire.

ICE CUBES

ONE PART BRANDY

ONE PART MADEIRA OR ANY SWEET, FORTIFIED WHITE WINE

THREE DROPS OF CURAÇAO

TWO DASHES OF ANGOSTURA BITTERS

CHILLED DRY CHAMPAGNE

A SLICE OF ORANGE

○ Place five ice cubes in a cocktail shaker and add the brandy, sweet wine, Curaçao and Angostura bitters.

○ Shake well and strain into a tall champagne flute. Fill it gently with champagne and garnish it with a slice of orange.

Right: Prince of Wales, a champagne-based cocktail.

Above: Dry sherry puts old English style at the heart of this little drink.

English Bolo

A 'bolo' is traditionally a mixture of spirits (usually rum) and fruit juices. This version is a gentler drink, with dry sherry in place of rum.

A SUGAR CUBE

A STICK OF CINNAMON

ONE PART LEMON JUICE

TWO PARTS DRY SHERRY

ICE AND SODA WATER (OPTIONAL)

❍ Crush the sugar cube, cinnamon and lemon juice together in a lowball glass, then simply add the sherry, stir and serve. Soda water and ice can be added to make a longer drink if preferred.

Scotch Frog

I have no idea how this rather punchy drink got its name. Perhaps it is rather like Welsh rarebit, which is reputed to be the poor Welsh householder's substitute for rabbit. But why should any self-respecting Scot want a substitute for a frog?

ICE CUBES

TWO PARTS VODKA

ONE PART GALLIANO

ONE PART COINTREAU

THE JUICE OF A LIME

A DASH OF ANGOSTURA BITTERS

MARASCHINO CHERRY JUICE OR CHERRY LIQUEUR

○ Place three ice cubes in a cocktail shaker and add the vodka, Galliano, Cointreau, lime juice, bitters and cherry juice or cherry liqueur.

○ Shake well and strain into a cocktail glass.

○ Serve ungarnished.

Left: The tartness of lime is offset by the sweetness of the liqueurs in the Scotch Frog.

Scotch Old-Fashioned

Here's a cocktail that adds a bittersweet touch to whisky. No doubt the Scots would disapprove strongly of any addition to what they believe is already the perfect drink, but if you're not Scottish you might like to try it.

A CUBE OF SUGAR

A FEW DASHES OF ANGOSTURA BITTERS

TWO MEASURES OF SCOTCH WHISKY

ICE CUBES

○ Soak a sugar cube in Angostura bitters and place it in the bottom of a lowball glass.

○ Add just enough water to dissolve the sugar and then pour in the measures of whisky. Stir gently and drop in two ice cubes.

Above: The Scotch Old-Fashioned, a classic cocktail, was created around 1900.

Left: This version of Scotch Mist is served hot.

Scotch Mist

The simplest version of Scotch Mist is simply Scotch on the rocks with a twist of lemon zest over it. This hot version is served in a teacup and is known, for some strange reason, as the 'English' Scotch mist. It's probably something to do with the tea.

ONE PART SCOTCH WHISKY

THREE PARTS FRESHLY BREWED CEYLON TEA

HONEY

THICK CREAM

- ❍ Mix the whisky and tea together and add the honey to taste, stirring over a low heat until almost (but not quite) boiling.

- ❍ Pour into small (demitasse) coffee cups and float a teaspoon of cream onto the surface of each drink.

Spirit of Scotland

Most appropriately named, as Drambuie is made of whisky, heather and honey. What could be more Scottish?

CRUSHED ICE

TWO PARTS SCOTCH WHISKY

ONE PART DRAMBUIE

HALF A PART LEMON JUICE

- ❍ Place a scoop of crushed ice in a blender or cocktail shaker and add the whisky, Drambuie and lemon juice.

- ❍ Blend everything together briskly and strain into a cocktail glass.

Right: The White Heather won an award in Hamburg, Germany in 1984.

Below: In Spirit of Scotland, two well-known products of Scotland are combined.

White Heather

Bartenders throughout the world compete regularly at international gatherings, where new drinks are tried, discussed and judged. This award-winning recipe, invented by barman Rodney Brock, specified the brand of each of the ingredients, but we leave it to readers to select their own. It really is a wonderful drink.

ICE CUBES

ONE PART SCOTCH WHISKY

ONE PART CRÈME DE BANANE

ONE PART CRÈME DE CACAO

TWO PARTS THIN CREAM

NUTMEG

○ Place three ice cubes in a cocktail shaker and add all the ingredients except the nutmeg.

○ Shake well and strain into a cocktail glass.

○ Grate nutmeg over the drink and serve.

Rob Roy

This drink, named after the famous Scottish hero, should be poured whenever a toast is drunk to heroes.

ICE CUBES

TWO DASHES OF ANGOSTURA BITTERS

ONE GENEROUS PART SCOTCH WHISKY

ONE EQUALLY GENEROUS PART SWEET VERMOUTH

A TWIST OF ORANGE

○ Place two ice cubes in a lowball glass and splash in two dashes of bitters.

○ Add the whisky and vermouth, garnish with a twist of orange and serve.

Above: Experts say this is absolutely the only drink to enjoy on St Andrew's Day. The Rob Roy should be made only with real Scotch.

Above: Blacksmith Cocktail, a smooth blend of Drambuie and crème de café.

Glasgow Cocktail

Scots purists will probably gasp in horror at the very thought of anybody adulterating their national drink in a cocktail, but this is an old Scottish favourite.

ICE CUBES

THREE PARTS SCOTCH WHISKY

ONE PART DRY VERMOUTH

A DASH OF LEMON JUICE

A DASH OF AMARETTO

○ Place five or six ice cubes in a cocktail shaker and add the other ingredients.

○ Shake well and strain into a lowball glass filled with ice cubes.

○ Serve ungarnished.

Blacksmith Cocktail

There's a rough Irish drink called a 'Blacksmith', which consists, predictably, of half a pint each of Guinness stout and barley wine, probably best drunk in the glow of the blacksmith's forge. Our Blacksmith Cocktail, however, is better suited to the cocktail bar.

ICE CUBES

ONE PART BRANDY

ONE PART DRAMBUIE

ONE PART CRÈME DE CAFÉ

○ Place four or five ice cubes in a bar mixing glass, add all the ingredients and stir well.

○ Serve on the rocks in a lowball glass or a whisky glass, ungarnished.

Highland Fling

Here's another whisky-based drink that will have the Scots purists fuming, but for us Sassenachs – and other foreign folk – it's a real pleasure.

ICE CUBES

TWO PARTS BLENDED SCOTCH WHISKY

ONE PART SWEET VERMOUTH

TWO DASHES OF ORANGE BITTERS

A GREEN OLIVE

○ Place three or four ice cubes in a shaker and add the whisky, vermouth and orange bitters.

○ Shake well and strain into a cocktail glass.

○ Garnish with the olive and serve.

Opposite: A heartwarming cocktail to sip on a misty Scottish night. Or any night, come to that.

Above: The Leprechaun is a merry little Irish drink which calls for a good measure of fine Irish whiskey.

Leprechaun

It is said that if you capture a leprechaun he will grant you a wish, but who could wish for more than this merry wee drink?

ICE CUBES

ONE PART IRISH WHISKEY (A LARGE ONE, OF COURSE)

TWO PARTS TONIC WATER

LEMON PEEL

○ Place two ice cubes in a highball glass and add the whiskey and tonic.

○ Stir reverently and twist the lemon peel over it.

○ Drop in the twisted peel and serve.

Irish Coffee

This is a fine alternative to ordinary coffee at the end of a good meal. The Irish have long been putting a dash of whiskey in their tea and calling it Irish tea, but the barman changed the recipe slightly to appeal to the American airmen who were using Shannon Airport as their base during World War II. Americans have always preferred coffee to tea.

You can actually buy an Irish liqueur called Irish Velvet, which is based on Irish whiskey, black coffee and sugar. It's not as pleasant, or as much fun, as making your own.

ONE PART IRISH WHISKEY

FIVE PARTS STRONG, BLACK COFFEE

A TEASPOON OF BROWN SUGAR

ONE PART THICK CREAM

○ Pour the Irish whiskey and hot coffee into a warmed Irish coffee glass, which is sometimes a goblet with a handle like a teacup and sometimes shaped like a large wineglass.

○ Add brown sugar to taste and stir gently until it is dissolved.

○ Trickle the cream over the back of a teaspoon onto the surface of the coffee.

Right: Irish Coffee was originally created by the bartender at Shannon Airport near the Irish coast in the late 1940s.

Clubman Cocktail

Irish Mist is a liqueur based on Irish whiskey flavoured with herbs and honey and produced in Tulach Mhor, Ireland. The Clubman is a very colourful drink, guaranteed to start the conversation flowing.

ICE CUBES

ONE PART IRISH MIST

FOUR PARTS ORANGE JUICE

A DESSERTSPOON OF EGG WHITE

A DASH OF BLUE CURAÇAO

○ Place four ice cubes in a cocktail shaker and add the Irish Mist, orange juice and egg white.

○ Shake briskly and strain into a lowball glass.

○ Carefully trickle the blue Curaçao down the sides of the glass (you might like to use a straw) to create a marbled effect.

Above: In the Clubman Cocktail, blue Curaçao is trickled down the sides of the glass to create the blue veins.

Colleen

Here's a pretty drink with which to toast a strong Irish lass. There's certainly nothing weak and frilly about it.

ICE CUBES

THREE PARTS IRISH WHISKEY

ONE PART COINTREAU

TWO PARTS IRISH MIST

A SPLASH OF FRESH LEMON JUICE

○ Place four or five ice cubes in a cocktail shaker and add all the ingredients.

○ Shake briskly and strain into a chilled cocktail glass.

Left: The French liqueur adds a continental touch to this essentially Irish drink.

Kerry Cooler

This is a sweet and warming drink for a chilly Irish evening. It can be enjoyed as a short or long drink, depending on the quantity of soda water used.

ICE CUBES

TWO PARTS IRISH WHISKEY

ONE PART DRY (FINO) SHERRY

ONE PART LEMON JUICE

HALF A PART OF ALMOND EXTRACT OR ORGEAT SYRUP

CLUB SODA WATER

SLICE OF LEMON

○ Place five or six cubes of ice in a shaker and add the whiskey, sherry, lemon juice and orgeat or almond extract.

○ Shake well and strain into a tall glass.

○ Top up the glass with soda water and garnish with a slice of lemon, slit and placed on the rim.

Left: They say the Kerry Cooler is a cure for colds, but why wait? Prevention is better than cure, as every Irishman knows.

Irish Blackthorn

The Irish blackthorn produces sloe berries, as used in sloe gin. So it's surprising that this cocktail contains no sloe gin. There's some real Irish logic in there somewhere.

TWO PARTS IRISH WHISKEY

ONE PART DRY VERMOUTH

THREE DASHES OF PERNOD

THREE DASHES OF ANGOSTURA BITTERS

CRUSHED ICE

ICE CUBES

○ Stir all the ingredients with a scoop of crushed ice in a suitable jug or large glass.

○ Fill a tall glass with ice cubes and strain the mixture over them.

○ Serve ungarnished.

Right: At the end of a long walk across the Irish countryside, the Blackthorn is the perfect cooler.

Above: It takes a steady hand to serve this unusual drink without causing a minor explosion.

Car Bomb

Part of the fun of this Irish drink is the novel way in which it is served. Like its namesake, it comes as a surprise. There you are, innocently sipping your Guinness, when an explosion of whiskey suddenly hits you.

ONE PINT OF GUINNESS

ONE PART BAILEY'S IRISH CREAM

ONE PART IRISH WHISKEY

○ Pour the Guinness into a large tankard.

○ Mix the whiskey and Irish cream in a shot glass and drop it – glass and all – into the tankard, where it will sink to the bottom.

○ As you drink, the shot glass tips over, sending a stream of whiskey and Irish cream into your mouth along with the Guinness.

Everybody's Irish Cocktail

This green drink is an ideal one to serve on St Patrick's Day, when even the beer is traditionally served green.

ICE CUBES

THREE PARTS IRISH WHISKEY

ONE PART GREEN CHARTREUSE

THREE DASHES OF GREEN CRÈME DE MENTHE

A GREEN OLIVE

○ Place four or five ice cubes in a bar glass and add the whiskey, Chartreuse and crème de menthe.

○ Stir well and strain into a chilled cocktail glass.

○ Garnish with the green olive on a cocktail stick.

Left: The green hills of Ireland are captured in your glass with this magical drink.

Pousse Café

In France, eating and drinking is regarded as a serious pastime and it is easy to see how this complex creation captured the imagination of Parisian gourmets. This is the original drink on which the modern 'shooter' is based. It requires a very steady hand to keep the colours separate.

ONE PART GRENADINE

ONE PART GREEN CRÈME DE MENTHE

ONE PART GALLIANO

ONE PART KÜMMEL

ONE PART BRANDY

○ Into a small, basically cylindrical glass, pour each of the ingredients in the order given, trickling them slowly over a spoon onto the surface of the previous layer until a pretty striped effect is achieved.

○ Serve carefully.

Right: Traditionally served after dinner, the Pousse Café can have as many layers of colour as you like.

The Sidecar

The 1920s, the golden age of the cocktail, was also the golden age of motoring. The novelty of the horseless carriage had not yet worn off and automobiles were different and dashing. And the most dashing of all the knights of the road were the gallant fellows who dared to ride motorcycles.

The Sidecar is said to be named after a rather eccentric military man who used to arrive at Harry's New York Bar in Paris in the sidecar of a chauffeur-driven motorcycle.

ICE CUBES

ONE AND A HALF PARTS BRANDY

ONE PART COINTREAU

ONE PART FRESH LEMON JUICE (OR MORE TO TASTE)

○ Place four ice cubes in a mixing glass, pour the ingredients over the ice and stir well.

○ Strain into a cocktail glass and serve.

Above: The Sidecar is one of many cocktail classics that had its origins in the legendary Harry's New York Bar in Paris.

Sazerac

This romantic drink derived its name from the company importing brandy from France, Sazerac du Forge et Fils. Later, rye whiskey replaced the brandy in the recipe, but the name remained the same.

A LUMP OF SUGAR

A DASH OF ANGOSTURA BITTERS

ICE CUBES

TWO GENEROUS PARTS RYE WHISKEY

A DASH OF PERNOD

A TWIST OF LEMON

○ Soak the sugar lump in Angostura bitters and place it in a cooled lowball glass with an ice cube.

○ Add the whiskey and stir well.

○ Add the Pernod and twist the lemon rind over the glass to serve.

Above: The romantic Sazerac originated in New Orleans.

Steeplejack

Calvados is distilled apple cider and is a popular spirit in parts of France, such as Normandy, where apple cider is the drink of the area. In other parts of the world it is sold as apple brandy or applejack.

ONE PART CALVADOS

ONE AND A HALF PARTS CHILLED APPLE JUICE

ONE AND A HALF PARTS SODA WATER

ONE TEASPOON OF LIME JUICE

ICE CUBES

A SLICE OF LEMON

○ Pour the Calvados, apple juice, soda water and lime juice into a bar glass and stir gently.

○ Pour the mixture into a highball glass and add enough ice to fill it.

○ Garnish with a slice of lemon.

Above: Steeplejack is a long cool drink with a distinct apple flavour.

Above: Between the Sheets is a drink to be shared with a very close friend.

Between the Sheets

Crisp and inviting as a freshly made bed, this delightful drink just cries out to be shared by lovers. And where better than in Paris, where love is always in the air?

ICE CUBES

ONE PART LIGHT RUM

ONE PART BRANDY

ONE PART COINTREAU

A TEASPOON OF LEMON JUICE

A TWIST OF LEMON RIND

○ Place five or six ice cubes in a cocktail shaker. Add the rum, brandy, Cointreau and lemon juice.

○ Shake well and strain into a cocktail glass.

○ Serve garnished with a twist of lemon rind.

The Bastille Bomb

Fire off this little shooter to celebrate the anniversary of the storming of the Bastille in Paris on July 14th, 1789.

ONE PART GRENADINE

ONE PART BLUE CURAÇAO

ONE PART COINTREAU

○ Start with the grenadine as a base in a small cylindrical glass, then trickle the Cointreau on top of it.

○ Round it off with a trickled layer of blue Curaçao. Voila!

Above: Part of the charm of a shooter is its colourful, layered appearance. Make sure you have a selection of brightly coloured drinks, such a cherry brandy, crème de menthe and green chartreuse, before setting out to create your own rainbow masterpiece.

kir royale

THIS DRINK WAS FIRST named Kir after the war hero and mayor of Dijon, Felix Kir. In smart cocktail bars the rough peasant wine was later replaced with fine champagne and the drink was elevated to royal status. Today Kir is the same drink made with dry white wine, while Kir Royale is the version that uses champagne.

SEVEN PARTS CHILLED DRY CHAMPAGNE
ONE PART CHILLED CRÈME DE CASSIS (OR RASPBERRY LIQUEUR IF YOU PREFER)
A TWIST OF LEMON RIND

- Fill a champagne flute about three-quarters full with chilled champagne.
- Add the liqueur and serve garnished with the twist of lemon rind.

Opposite Kir Royale, an old classic, is said to have been made originally by Burgundian farm labourers.

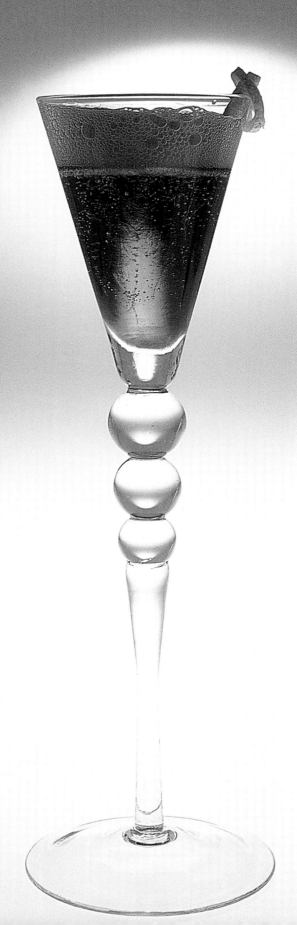

French 75

Cocktails have been made to celebrate all kinds of things. In World War I the French light field gun, known as the '75', was regarded as one of the world's most formidable weapons. After the War, when veterans gathered in Harry's New York Bar in Paris, a special cocktail was devised to remember the fierce field gun.

ONE PART CHILLED LONDON DRY GIN

TWO DASHES OF SWEET GOMME SYRUP

CHILLED DRY CHAMPAGNE

A TWIST OF LEMON

○ In a champagne flute or cocktail glass, pour a measure of gin and add the two dashes of gomme syrup.

○ Top up with champagne.

○ Garnish with the twist of lemon.

Above: Named after the famous French field gun, the French 75 is another classic cocktail from Harry's New York Bar in Paris.

A Shot of French Fire

Here's a colourful little drink with a French flavour and a cheerful appearance.

ONE PART GREEN CHARTREUSE

ONE PART MARASCHINO LIQUEUR

ONE PART CHERRY BRANDY

ONE PART KÜMMEL

○ Starting with the chartreuse, trickle each of the ingredients over the back of a spoon into a small, straight-sided glass in the order shown.

○ Admire for a few seconds, and toss it down in a single, multi-coloured gulp.

Calvados Cocktail

Calvados is the spirit distilled from apple cider and is one of the chief spirit drinks made in Normandy, France's cider country.

ICE CUBES

ONE PART CALVADOS

ONE PART FRESH ORANGE JUICE

ONE PART COINTREAU

A SPLASH OF ORANGE BITTERS

A TWIST OF ORANGE RIND

○ Place five or six ice cubes in a shaker and add all the ingredients.

○ Shake briskly and strain into a chilled cocktail glass.

○ Garnish with the twist of orange rind and serve.

Above: The Calvados Cocktail is made only from fruit-based drinks. What could be more healthy?

bellini

THE BELLINI BECAME the favourite drink of celebrities like Noël Coward and Ernest Hemingway when they visited Harry's Bar in Venice. It's easy to see why.

Modern bartenders may be tempted to use the readily available canned or boxed peach juice for this drink, but the real connoisseur would never accept anything but the fresh juice of ripe peaches. It really is worth the extra effort.

Peel several ripe peaches and remove the stones. Place them in a blender and whip them to a smooth purée.

ONE GENEROUS PART FRESH PEACH JUICE
FOUR EQUALLY GENEROUS PARTS DRY CHAMPAGNE
A PEACH SLICE

- Pour the fruit juice into a champagne flute, filling it about a quarter full.
- Top up the glass with champagne. Do not stir or shake.
- Garnish with the peach slice on the rim of the glass and serve.

Opposite: The Bellini was created in the 1940s by Guiseppe Cipriani, the founder of Harry's Bar in Venice, in honour of the famous Venetian painter, Bellini.

La Jolla

This is a passionate concoction based on that most fiery of Italian spirits, grappa. Drink it with caution!

ICE CUBES

THREE PARTS GRAPPA

ONE PART CRÈME DE BANANE

ONE PART LEMON JUICE

A SPLASH OF ORANGE JUICE

A SLICE OF ORANGE

○ Place four ice cubes in a cocktail shaker, add the grappa, crème de banane, lemon juice and orange juice and shake well.

○ Strain into a cocktail glass and decorate with a slice of lemon.

Left: The grappa turns a sweet little fruit drink into a fiery glass of Italian passion.

Above: The Montgomery was invented by Ernest Hemingway in honour of the famous British general of World War II.

Frangelico Luau

Frangelico is reputed to have been created by an Italian hermit three centuries ago and is a delicious liqueur made from hazelnuts and berries. It is the base for many unusual and complex-flavoured cocktails like this one.

ONE PART FRANGELICO LIQUEUR

FOUR PARTS FRESH PINEAPPLE JUICE

A DASH OF GRENADINE

ICE CUBES

FRESH PINEAPPLE

Montgomery

This is a variation of the martini, originally invented by Ernest Hemingway in Harry's Bar in Venice. During World War II, Hemingway claimed Field Marshall Montgomery would fight the enemy only if he had 15 soldiers to every one of theirs. He decided this was a good proportion of gin to vermouth.

Today Harry's version is slightly modified and has become a speciality of the bar.

TEN PARTS GIN

ONE PART DRY VERMOUTH

- ○ Mix the gin and vermouth in a bar glass and pour into as many martini glasses as you are preparing.
- ○ Place them in a freezer and leave until frozen solid.
- ○ Serve frozen, so they can be sipped very slowly as they thaw.

- ○ Pour the Frangelico, pineapple juice and grenadine into a blender and blend for about 10 seconds.
- ○ Pour into a chilled tall glass and add three ice cubes.
- ○ Decorate with a slice of fresh pineapple.

Right: Frangelico Luau provides a rich combination of fruit, berry and nut flavours.

B & B

This is a natural combination, as Benedictine is a herb-flavoured liqueur based on brandy and originally made by Benedictine monks; they claimed it had fine medicinal qualities, which it probably does.

ICE CUBES

ONE PART BRANDY

ONE PART BENEDICTINE

A TWIST OF LIME

○ Place two or three ice cubes in a bar glass and add the brandy and Benedictine.

○ Stir well and strain into a small cocktail glass.

○ Garnish with the twist of lime.

B & B Collins

The B & B can be extended to make a B & B Collins simply by adding soda, but that would be very unadventurous. Rather, try this little variation.

CRUSHED ICE

TWO PARTS BRANDY

THE JUICE OF HALF A LEMON

A TEASPOON OF SUGAR SYRUP

CLUB SODA WATER

ONE PART BENEDICTINE

A SLICE OF LEMON

○ Add three scoops of crushed ice to a bar glass and mix in the brandy, lemon juice and sugar syrup.

○ Strain into a chilled lowball glass and top with soda water.

○ Now carefully float the Benedictine on the surface and garnish with the slice of lemon.

Opposite: B & B is a natural blend of brandy and Benedictine, a herb-flavoured brandy liqueur made in Normandy, France.

Espresso Royale

Espresso coffee was invented in Italy as a fine way to taste good strong coffee without having to swallow a whole cup of it. Espresso Royal turns the coffee into a memorable event that can also be served as a dessert.

ONE PART SUGAR

TWO PARTS WATER

ONE PART STRONG ESPRESSO COFFEE

ONE PART TIA MARIA OR KAHLUA

WHIPPED CREAM

○ Dissolve the sugar in the warmed water, add the espresso and allow to cool.

○ Chill until almost frozen.

○ Pour into a chilled wine glass and top with Tia Maria and whipped cream before serving.

Right: The fresh whipped cream adds the crown to this king of coffee drinks.

Galliano Hot Shot

Italy is the home of strong espresso coffee and also the sweet delight known as Galliano. It's natural the two should meet in this intriguing taste combination. If the coffee is very hot, it may be advisable to sip this drink, rather than tossing it back in a single gulp.

ONE PART GALLIANO

ONE PART VERY STRONG, HOT COFFEE

THICK CREAM

○ Half-fill a shot glass with Galliano and carefully trickle about the same quantity of hot coffee over the back of a teaspoon to form a dark layer on it.

○ Finally, add a topping of cream, sliding it carefully onto the surface of the coffee.

Above: Galliano Hot Shot is an intriguing combination of Galliano and hot coffee.

Above: Galliano is a golden-hued Italian liqueur that is used in many well-known cocktails, in particular the Harvey Wallbanger (page 34).

Danish Mary

In the chilly Scandinavian countries they distill a robust liquor called aquavit. It is made from potatoes or grain and lightly flavoured with caraway and other seeds. Traditionally it is enjoyed neat and swallowed in a single gulp, but it can also be used in some good cocktails.

ICE CUBES

ONE PART AQUAVIT

ONE SMALL CAN OF TOMATO JUICE

TWO DASHES OF WORCESTERSHIRE SAUCE

LEMON JUICE

CELERY SALT

A CELERY STICK

○ Place four or five ice cubes in a cocktail shaker and add the aquavit, tomato juice, Worcestershire sauce, a few teaspoons of lemon juice and a dusting of celery salt.

○ Shake well and strain into a highball glass.

○ Garnish with the stick of celery and serve.

Right: The Danish Mary is a Bloody Mary made with aquavit instead of vodka.

Kempinski Cocktail

This refreshing cocktail probably originated in the Hotel Kempinski in Berlin, where it got its name, although the ingredients are not particularly German.

ONE PART BACARDI RUM

ONE PART COINTREAU

TWO PARTS GRAPEFRUIT JUICE

CRUSHED ICE

A MARASCHINO CHERRY

○ Shake the rum, Cointreau and grapefruit juice with a scoop of crushed ice in a cocktail shaker.

○ Strain it into a cocktail glass.

○ Garnish with a cherry and serve.

Right: Grapefruit juice gives this attractive drink its refreshingly bitter flavour, making it an ideal summer lunchtime cocktail.

Apple Ginger Punch

Ginger adds a glowing touch of spicy warmth to this drink, as does the Calvados – perfect for a chilly winter's evening in Northern Europe.

A LARGE BLOCK OF ICE

ONE BOTTLE OF CALVADOS

HALF A CUP OF MARASCHINO LIQUEUR

HALF A CUP OF KIRSCH

A BOTTLE OF GINGER WINE

THREE CUPS OF PINEAPPLE OR GRAPEFRUIT JUICE

FOUR APPLES (RED OR GREEN)

THREE BOTTLES OF GINGER BEER

- ❍ Place the ice in a punch bowl and pour the Calvados, maraschino, Kirsch, ginger wine and fruit juice over it.
- ❍ Cut the apples into wedge-shaped slices and float them in the punch.
- ❍ Shortly before serving, add the ginger beer to the bowl.

Right: Apple Ginger Punch, a cheerful and refreshing party punch, is filled with apple flavour from several sources and ginger to give it an exciting little bite.

Cranberry Splash

The Dutch island of Terschelling has become famous for its cranberries and cranberry products – from cranberry teas to jams and syrups. It is natural that they use these delicious berries in drinks, too.

ICE CUBES

ONE PART VODKA

FOUR PARTS CRANBERRY JUICE

SLICE OF LIME

- ❍ Fill a tall glass with ice cubes, add the vodka and cranberry juice and stir gently.
- ❍ Garnish with a slice of lime after squeezing a little of the zest from the skin over the drink.

Above: The tangy taste of cranberries gives this drink a fresh summer flavour.

Above: Don't be fooled by the innocent twist of lemon, this Scandinavian cloud packs a thunderous punch.

Northern Cloud

Cloudberry liqueur is a delicious drink produced in Finland. All the Scandinavian countries have a tradition of drinking fiery schnapps or akvavit to keep out the chills, so the two drinks combine well as a winter warmer.

ONE PART CLOUDBERRY LIQUEUR

ONE PART AKVAVIT

ICE CUBES

TWIST OF LEMON PEEL

○ Stir the cloudberry liqueur and akvavit together in a bar glass.

○ Place three of four ice cubes in a cocktail glass and pour the cocktail over them.

○ Squeeze the lemon peel over the drink and drop the twist in as garnish before serving.

Cranberry Vodka

As cranberries are so plentiful in Holland, it is to be expected that they find their away into interesting cocktail recipes. This one uses whole berries and takes three days to make. It's worth the wait, though.

ONE KILO OF FRESH CRANBERRIES

A BOTTLE OF GOOD QUALITY VODKA

ICE CUBES

○ Fill a large glass jar with fresh cranberries and top up with vodka. Seal and leave, turning over morning and evening for three days.

○ Remove most of the fruit and place the jar in the fridge.

○ To serve, fill a cocktail glass – or wine glass – with ice cubes and pour the cranberry vodka over them.

Above: Cranberry Vodka is a delicious liqueur you can create in your own kitchen. The three-day wait is well worth it.

Above: The frothy gloss provided by the egg white makes this a blonde every gentleman will prefer.

Dutch Blonde

The Dutch produce their gin in several different styles, all of which add interesting dimensions to good cocktails.

ICE CUBES

TWO PARTS JONGE GENEVER (YOUNG DUTCH GIN)

ONE PART COINTREAU

TWO PARTS PINEAPPLE JUICE

THE WHITE OF ONE EGG

○ Place four or five ice cubes in a cocktail shaker and add the gin, Cointreau, pineapple juice and egg white.

○ Shake well until the drink has a silky sheen and strain into a chilled cocktail glass.

○ Serve ungarnished.

Sangria

Sangria is one of the old traditional punches, much enjoyed in Spanish-speaking countries. The name is derived from the Spanish *sangre*, meaning blood, and obviously refers to its colour. There are almost as many recipes for sangria as there are for martinis. Interestingly, sangria is one of the few punches that are made as an individual drink as well as a communal cocktail. We have used large quantities here, but you can scale them down to suit your own needs.

A nice touch is to serve the sangria in a goblet with a sugar-frosted rim. It turns the drink into a really special occasion.

TWO BOTTLES OF RED WINE

HALF A CUP OF CURAÇAO

HALF A CUP OF BRANDY

THE JUICE OF AN ORANGE

THE JUICE OF A LEMON OR LIME

HALF A CUP OF CASTER SUGAR (OR TO TASTE)

A CHUNK OF ICE

ORANGE, PEACH AND LEMON SLICES

A SMALL BOTTLE OF SODA WATER (OPTIONAL)

○ Mix all the liquid ingredients, except the soda water.

○ Add the caster sugar and strain into a punch bowl containing a chunk of ice.

○ Garnish with the fruit slices.

○ Add the soda water shortly before serving.

Fandango

Named after the dance, this is a merry drink to get the feet tapping to the rhythm of a Spanish guitar.

ICE CUBES

TWO PARTS DRY FINO SHERRY

ONE PART LIGHT RUM

TWO DASHES OF ORANGE BITTERS

A COCKTAIL CHERRY

○ Place five or six ice cubes in a shaker, add the sherry, rum and orange bitters and shake well.

○ Strain into a chilled cocktail glass and serve garnished with a cherry.

Right: This crisp, fresh-flavoured cocktail dances a merry fandango on your tongue. It's the perfect aperitif.

Sherry Flip

Oloroso is a medium-dry style of sherry with a pleasantly nutty flavour. Originally from Spain, sherry-style wines are now made in several other countries, although the name 'sherry' is protected under EU regulations and can only be used for the Spanish product.

ICE CUBES

ONE SHERRY GLASS OF OLOROSO SHERRY

ONE WHOLE EGG

ONE TABLESPOON OF CASTER SUGAR

GRATED NUTMEG

○ Place five or six ice cubes in a cocktail shaker and add the sherry, egg and caster sugar.

○ Shake very well until the mixture is smooth and silky.

○ Strain into a cocktail glass and sprinkle with a little grated nutmeg before serving.

Above: The Sherry Flip is a good drink to have with brunch, in place of the more usual champagne and orange cocktail.

Cava Breakfast Cocktail

The best Spanish sparkling wines are made in the traditional method known as 'cava'. This makes an ideal base for a refreshing summer breakfast drink (or for any time, for that matter).

ONE PART SPANISH BRANDY

ONE SLICE OF RIPE PEACH

THREE PARTS FRESH CHILLED SEVILLE ORANGE JUICE

FOUR PARTS WELL CHILLED CAVA SPARKLING WINE.

○ Pour a little brandy in the bottom of a Champagne flute and add the slice of ripe peach. Ideally this should be done the evening before the cocktail is to be served, to allow the peach to be infused with brandy.

○ Just before serving, add orange juice to fill the glass to about the halfway mark, and then top up gently with the cava sparkling wine, stir very lightly once and serve.

Left: Not many cocktails are designed for drinking in the morning, but this one certainly starts the day with a bang.

Cadiz

It seems natural that sherry forms the basic ingredient of many Spanish based cocktails. This one uses a dry fino sherry.

ICE CUBES

TWO PARTS FINO SHERRY

TWO PARTS BLACKBERRY BRANDY

ONE PART TRIPLE SEC

ONE PART FRESH CREAM

○ Place four or five ice cubes in a cocktail shaker and add all the ingredients.

○ Shake well and strain into a whisky glass filled with ice cubes.

○ Serve ungarnished.

Below: This creamy little sherry-based drink makes a good finale to a convivial meal.

Greek Coffee

This is the Greek equivalent of Irish coffee and it makes a fine finish to a good Greek meal.

ONE PART METAXA BRANDY

A SPLASH OF TIA MARIA

A CUP OF HOT, VERY STRONG BLACK COFFEE

A GENEROUS SPOON OF THICK CREAM

○ Pour the brandy and Tia Maria into a heavy mug or Irish coffee glass, and stir in the hot coffee.

○ Carefully spoon the cream on top of the cocktail, trying to create a clean separating line between the dark and light parts.

○ Serve piping hot.

The Greek Tiger

This variation of the classic cocktail called the Tiger Tail was offered to me on a ferry from Athens to Poros. The ship's steward insisted it was the perfect way to introduce a foreigner to the delights of ouzo – a popular Greek drink with a pleasant liqorice flavour, which turns milky white when mixed with water. I had to agree.

ICE CUBES

FOUR PARTS FRESH ORANGE JUICE

ONE PART OUZO

A SLICE OF LIME

A TWIST OF LIME PEEL

○ Place four ice cubes in a cocktail shaker and add the orange juice and ouzo.

○ Shake well and strain into a cocktail glass.

○ Squeeze the slice of lime over the drink and decorate it with the lime peel.

Opposite: Greek Coffee is traditionally made strong and dark. This version adds a touch of Greek drama.

Ouzo Cooler

Aniseed and orange flavours blend easily in this pleasant summer drink, which can be made as strong or weak as you please.

ONE PART OUZO

TWO PARTS CHILLED ORANGE JUICE

A SQUEEZE OF LEMON

CHILLED SODA WATER

○ Pour the ouzo and orange juice into a tall glass.

○ Top up with soda water and squeeze the lemon over it.

○ Stir gently and add a twist of lemon rind as garnish before serving.

Left: Ouzo Cooler – a drink to remind you of those lazy days on your favourite Greek island.

Black Cossack

Why anybody should want to mess with Guinness, goodness knows. But this is a simple drink and popular in some parts.

A LARGE SLUG OF VODKA

A GLASS OF GUINNESS STOUT

○ Simply pour the vodka carefully into the stout and drink it. Don't stir or shake it, as the froth would be overwhelming.

Right: The Black Cossack is a stunningly simple combination of vodka and Guinness.

Russian Coffee

The Russians have the reputation not only of making the best vodka but also of being able to drink it in large quantities. And who needs ordinary coffee when there's a drink as warming as this one to keep out the Siberian chill? Names and styles vary from bartender to bartender.

ONE PART VODKA

ONE PART COFFEE LIQUEUR (TIA MARIA OR KAHLUA)

ONE PART THIN CREAM

HALF A CUP OF CRUSHED ICE

COCOA POWDER (OPTIONAL)

○ Place all the ingredients in a blender and give them a brisk whirl for about 10 seconds.

○ Pour the result into a chilled champagne saucer and decorate with a swirl of cream.

○ You could also sprinkle a dusting of cocoa powder on the surface for added flavour.

The Volga Boatman

I doubt whether any Volga boatman could have afforded this delightful drink, unless his boat happened to be an elegant pleasure craft, but it's a delightfully cheerful drink.

CRUSHED ICE

ONE PART VODKA

ONE PART CHERRY BRANDY

ONE PART FRESH ORANGE JUICE

A MARASCHINO CHERRY

○ Place three spoons of crushed ice in a cocktail shaker and add the vodka, cherry brandy and orange juice.

○ Shake well and strain into a cocktail glass.

○ Garnish with the cherry on a cocktail stick and serve.

Moscow Mule

You can now buy ready-mixed Moscow Mules in cans, but it's far more fun to make your own, complete with your own variations and personal touches. When it comes to cocktails, creativity is the name of the game.

ICE CUBES

ONE GENEROUS PART VODKA

A TEASPOON OF LIME JUICE

GINGER BEER

A SLICE OF FRESH LIME

❍ Place two ice cubes in a chilled highball glass and pour in the vodka and lime juice.

❍ Stir well and fill with ginger beer.

❍ Garnish with the lime and serve.

Above: The Moscow Mule demonstrates how vodka teams up with any fruit flavours.

white russian

THIS SMOOTH WHITE cocktail probably reminded its inventor of the glistening snow of

Siberia. It's certainly a great comforter on a frosty night.

CRUSHED ICE
ONE PART VODKA
ONE PART WHITE CRÈME DE CACAO
ONE PART THICK CREAM

○ Place two spoons of crushed ice in a cocktail
shaker and add the vodka, crème de cacao and
cream.

○ Shake well and strain into a chilled cocktail
glass and serve ungarnished.

Opposite: The White Russian, a rich and creamy drink for a
chilly evening, is one of those deliciously dangerous drinks that
will last you the whole evening.

The Kremlin Colonel

This simple vodka-based creation was considered good enough for promotion to the highest rank.

CRUSHED ICE

TWO PARTS VODKA

HALF A PART FRESH LIME JUICE

A TEASPOON OF SUGAR (OR TO TASTE)

MINT LEAVES

○ Place a spoon of ice in a cocktail shaker and add the vodka, lime juice and sugar.

○ Shake well and strain into a cocktail glass.

○ Tear the mint leaves to release the aroma and drop them on to the drink as garnish.

Above: Undoubtedly Russian in origin and style, the Soviet is a punchy little drink.

The Soviet

Like the cuddly Russian bear, this vodka drink is stronger than it looks.

CRUSHED ICE

THREE PARTS VODKA

ONE PART SWEET SHERRY

ONE PART DRY VERMOUTH

LEMON PEEL

○ Place a scoop of crushed ice in a shaker, add the vodka, sherry and vermouth and shake well.

○ Strain into a cocktail glass and serve garnished with the lemon peel.

Above: The Kremlin Colonel ranks high in the vodka cocktail hierarchy.

Above: The Black Marble has the elegant simplicity of a good dry martini.

The Black Marble

Like many of the great classics of the cocktail world, the Black Marble is uncomplicated, but very chic. Poles and Russians traditionally enjoy their vodka neat, and this is about as close to that as you can get.

ICE CUBES

A LARGE BLACK OLIVE

ONE PART GOOD POLISH OR RUSSIAN VODKA

A SLICE OF ORANGE

○ Fill a lowball glass or wine goblet with ice cubes. Place the black olive right in the centre and pour the vodka over it.

○ Serve garnished with a slice of fresh orange.

Czarina

The Russians are known for their hard-drinking style. The country's First Lady was no exception, if we are to believe this was her favourite tipple; it packs a hefty kick.

ICE CUBES

TWO PARTS VODKA

ONE PART DRY VERMOUTH

ONE PART APRICOT BRANDY

DASH OF ANGOSTURA BITTERS

○ Place five or six ice cubes in a cocktail shaker and add all the ingredients.

○ Shake well and strain into a cocktail glass.

○ Serve ungarnished.

Left: The Czarina may be an elegant lady, but her charms conceal a powerful nature.

Cossack

The Cossacks who guarded the borders of Eastern Europe were hard-riding and hard-drinking warriors. They would probably have enjoyed this racy drink.

CRUSHED ICE

ONE PART BRANDY

ONE PART RUSSIAN VODKA

ONE PART FRESH LIME JUICE

HALF A TEASPOON OF CASTER SUGAR

❍ Place a scoop of crushed ice in a shaker and add all the ingredients.

❍ Shake and strain into a cocktail glass.

❍ Serve ungarnished.

Right: Warming brandy, cooling vodka and crisp lime add up to the perfect flavour balance of the Cossack.

Chocolate Black Russian

This may not be an authentic Russian drink, but the chocolate and vodka remind us of the heady days of the Russian Czars.

TWO PARTS KAHLUA

ONE PART VODKA

THREE PARTS SOFT CHOCOLATE ICE CREAM

○ Blend ingredients together and serve in a goblet. You may like to sprinkle a dusting of chocolate powder over the top before serving.

Left: Chocolate has always been considered a luxurious, pampering drink. This version adds power to that passion.

Katinka

Traditionally, the national drink of Russia – vodka – is taken neat and gulped fast. This cocktail softens the blow, tastes very refreshing and would probably be regarded as slightly effeminate in certain Russian circles.

CRUSHED ICE

TWO PARTS VODKA

ONE PART CHERRY BRANDY

LEMON JUICE TO TASTE

SLICE OF LEMON

○ Place a scoop of crushed ice in a shaker and add the vodka, cherry brandy and squeeze of lemon.

○ Shake well and strain into a cocktail glass.

○ Garnish with a slice of lemon, slit to fit over the side of the glass.

Below: The cherry brandy gives the Katinka a rich warm glow, very inviting on a Russian winter's night.

africa

Until recently, Africa's people rarely mixed their drinks, preferring plain beer or wine in various forms. Lately, however, enterprising African companies have produced a range of exciting new drinks based on local fruits, berries, melons and nuts, which have found their way into many charming local cocktails.

Elephant's Ear

Amarula Cream is a creamy liqueur made from African Marula Berries. At the end of summer, the berries fall from the trees and ferment on the ground, where they are eaten by elephants. The elephants' resulting drunken behaviour is very comical to behold.

ONE PART AMARULA CREAM

ONE PART CAPE BRANDY

TWO PARTS THIN CREAM

CRUSHED ICE

DRIED MANGO

A STRAW

○ Shake liquid ingredients with the crushed ice.

○ Strain into a lowball glass and garnish with a two slivers of dried mango (ears) and a straw (trunk).

Right: Fermenting marula berries have charmed Africa's elephants for centuries. Now they're ours to enjoy.

Prickly Pride

The prickly pear is the fruit of a broad-leafed cactus plant and is often boiled down to make a sweet, thin syrup not unlike maple syrup. It's a natural sweetener for African cocktails.

Cane spirit is a fiery white liquor distilled from the sugar cane grown in sub-tropical regions.

CRUSHED ICE

ONE PART CANE SPIRIT

ONE PART PRICKLY PEAR SYRUP

TWO PARTS CLUB SODA

TWIST OF LEMON PEEL

○ Place a scoop of crushed ice in a cocktail shaker and add the Cane spirit and prickly pear syrup.

○ Shake well and strain into a lowball glass.

○ Gently stir in the club soda and garnish with a twist of lemon peel before serving.

Right: If your local supermarket doesn't stock prickly pear syrup, you may have to visit Africa to sample this unusual drink.

Banana Bouncer

The ingredients for this delicious drink are all popular – and plentiful – in African countries.

ONE SHOT GLASS OF CAPE BRANDY

ONE EGG WHITE

ONE CUP OF COCONUT MILK

ONE TEASPOON HONEY

ONE VERY RIPE BANANA

CRUSHED ICE

○ Place the liquid ingredients, plus the honey and banana, in a blender.

○ Blend to smooth froth.

○ Serve over crushed ice in a tall glass.

Left: The Banana Bouncer is a whole meal in a glass. What a great start to the day!

Katembe

An unusual combination of flavours, which may not suit European palates, but is very popular in Mozambique.

ICE CUBES

ONE PART COLA

ONE PART DRY RED WINE

○ Place three or four ice cubes in a tall glass.

○ Add the cola and red wine and stir gently to mix the two, but no more.

○ Serve ungarnished.

Right: The Katembe was probably created originally to mask the flavour of some of Africa's very cheap wines of dubious quality.

Above: A wave of this wonderful wand will cure almost any woes.

Witchdoctor's Wand

In rural areas of Africa, the witchdoctor still holds sway over his people. This drink, while not made by the traditional herbalist, is said to have amazing restorative effects.

ONE PART CANE SPIRIT

TWO PARTS HONEY LIQUEUR

JUICE OF HALF A LEMON

ICE CUBES

❍ Stir the Cane spirit, honey liqueur and lemon juice well in a bar glass.

❍ Fill a cocktail glass with ice cubes and pour the mixed drink over them before serving.

Badger Bait

Honey badgers are becoming an endangered species in parts of Africa, where they are sometimes destroyed because they rob the hives of local beekeepers. Many conservation-aware producers now label their products 'Badger-friendly' and continue to produce their richly flavoured African honey products in a gentler way.

CRUSHED ICE

TWO PARTS HONEY LIQUEUR

ONE PART CAPE BRANDY

THREE PARTS FRESH ORANGE JUICE

SLICE OF LEMON

○ Place a scoop of crushed ice in a shaker and add the honey liqueur, brandy and orange juice.

○ Shake well and strain into a cocktail glass.

○ Squeeze the lemon slice over the drink and use the remainder as garnish.

Above: You'll find it's not only badgers that enjoy the rich honey flavour of this sweet cocktail.

Colonial Cocktail

Throughout the British Empire, London gin was the accepted link with the 'Old Country' and was enjoyed in large quantities from Kenya to Calcutta. This drink was found in a collection of cocktail recipes from a Nairobi club bar.

THREE PARTS LONDON DRY GIN

ONE PART FRESH GRAPEFRUIT JUICE

THREE DASHES OF MARASCHINO LIQUEUR

A GREEN OLIVE

ICE CUBES

❍ Place all the ingredients in a cocktail shaker with four or five cubes of ice and shake well.

❍ Strain into a martini glass and garnish with the green olive on a toothpick before serving.

Above: The colonies may have gone, but the echoes of London drinking linger on in bars all over the world.

Kenyan Coffee Cocktail

Based on a Kenyan coffee flavoured liqueur called Kenyan Gold, this is the perfect African sundowner.

CRUSHED ICE

TWO PARTS KENYAN GOLD

TWO PARTS FRESH CREAM

ONE PART BRANDY

GROUND CINNAMON

TWIST OF LIME RIND

○ Place a scoop of crushed ice in a shaker and add the liquid ingredients.

○ Shake well and strain into a cocktail glass.

○ Add a light dusting of cinnamon and garnish with a sliver of lime rind.

Right: For an exciting end to a meal, try this creamy cocktail as a sweet sauce over chocolate ice-cream.

Kenya Siku Kuu

Wherever people grow sugar cane, they make some form of rum. Kenya is no exception and Kenya's white rum is among the best in the world. Naturally it is the basis for several local cocktails. 'Siku Kuu' is the Kenyan term for 'Christmas'.

CRUSHED ICE

ONE PART KENYAN WHITE RUM

ONE PART COINTREAU

TWO PARTS GRANADILLA JUICE

SLICE OF ORANGE

MARASCHINO CHERRY

SPRIG OF MINT

❍ Place a scoop of crushed ice in a cocktail shaker and add the rum, Cointreau and granadilla juice.

❍ Shake well and strain into a cocktail glass, garnish with the orange slice, cherry and sprig of mint.

Opposite: The granadilla juice adds an unusual texture to this fruity African drink.

Above: Out of Africa – African sunshine is captured in this refreshing citrus-flavoured cocktail.

Out of Africa

Inspired by the book (and film), this is a tangy and refreshing antidote to the heat of the African veld. Cane spirit is a clear drink made from sugar cane and Van der Hum is a traditional South African liqueur made from tangerines.

ONE PART CANE SPIRIT

ONE PART VAN DER HUM

JUICE OF ONE ORANGE

JUICE OF HALF A GRAPEFRUIT

TWO PARTS APPLE JUICE

A GENEROUS DASH OF GRENADINE SYRUP (OR TO TASTE)

ICE CUBES

SLICE OF PINEAPPLE

❍ Place all the ingredients in a cocktail shaker with five or six ice cubes, shake well and strain into a lowball glass.

❍ Garnish with a slice of pineapple and serve.

Above: Dom Pedro is a stunningly simple combination of ice cream and whisky.

Dom Pedro

This has become a firm favourite in South Africa and appears there on many restaurant menus. The strange thing about it is that nobody seems to know who Dom Pedro was or how this sweet delight got its name. There are two basic versions, one using whisky and the other using Kahlua. Both are delicious.

VANILLA ICE CREAM

A GENEROUS MEASURE OF WHISKY OR KAHLUA

CHOCOLATE VERMICELLI

❍ Fill a lowball glass or goblet with soft vanilla ice cream and pour the whisky or Kahlua over.

❍ Whip briskly with a fork until well blended and serve garnished with a sprinkling of chocolate vermicelli. It is usual to provide a long bar spoon to help reach the bottom bits.

Above: The Green and Gold is a South African invention based on the colours of the national rugby team. Like the players it represents, this cocktail has a powerful kick.

Green and Gold

Inspired by the traditional sporting colours of South Africa's national teams, this is an attractive and rather pleasant little shooter.

ONE PART PASSION FRUIT SYRUP

ONE PART GREEN CRÈME DE MENTHE

A TEASPOON OF OUZO

○ Pour a little passion fruit syrup into the bottom of a shot glass or liqueur glass. Gently add the crème de menthe without letting the two colours mix.

○ When the glass is almost full, dribble a teaspoon of ouzo on top of the drink.

Left: Experiment with proportions to create your own version of the Wine Collins.

Wine Collins

As with many successful drinks, this one depends on achieving just the right balance between sweet and sour. In South Africa it is made using the local honey-sweet, fortified Muscadel wine, but any sweet, fortified wine will do.

ICE CUBES

FOUR PARTS MADEIRA, MARSALA OR RUBY PORT

HALF A PART FRESH LIME JUICE

DRY LEMON DRINK

A MARASCHINO CHERRY

○ Place four ice cubes in a mixing glass and add the wine and lime juice. Stir well and strain into a lowball glass.

○ Top up with the dry lemon drink. Stir lightly to retain the sparkle and garnish with the cherry on a stick.

Mampoer Mengelmoes

'Mampoer' is a rough liquor distilled (sometimes illegally) in the eastern part of South Africa from the juice of fermented ripe peaches. The word 'mengelmoes' simply means 'mixture' in Afrikaans.

ONE PART MAMPOER (OR ANY PEACH BRANDY)

ONE PART APRICOT LIQUEUR

THREE PARTS SODA WATER

ICE CUBES

○ In a bar glass, mix the liquids, stirring gently to retain the bubbles in the soda water.

○ Place four ice cubes in a tumbler and pour the cocktail mixture over them.

○ Serve ungarnished.

Opposite: You'll probably have to find a home distiller to obtain the ingredients of this typically rural African drink.

Above: Two of South Africa's most popular flavours combine to create this warming cocktail.

Brandy-Hum

South Africa's oldest liqueur is a golden spirit drink flavoured with tangerine peel and known as Van der Hum. Add to this the fact that brandy is the country's most popular spirit drink and you'll know why Brandy-Hum is a favourite local drink.

ONE PART VAN DER HUM LIQUEUR

ONE PART CAPE BRANDY

ICE CUBES

TWIST OF ORANGE PEEL

○ Stir the Van der Hum and brandy together in a cocktail mixing glass.

○ Fill a wine goblet with ice cubes and pour the cocktail mixture over them.

○ Squeeze the orange peel over the drink to release a fine spray of citrus zest, and drop a twist of the peel into the drink as garnish.

Mango Sunrise

Although the mango is indigenous to India, it is now widely grown in all sub-tropical regions, including parts of Africa, and its juice is a delicious base for fruity cocktails.

Mango Sunrise is becoming a popular brunch drink in Africa, where mid-morning parties are beginning to take the place of lunches, because of the fierce midday heat. South Africa also produces fine sparkling wines and brandies, so this is a natural cocktail for the region.

ONE SLICE OF RIPE MANGO

ONE PART BRANDY

TWO PARTS FRESH MANGO JUICE, CHILLED

THREE PARTS DRY SPARKLING WINE

A MARASCHINO CHERRY

○ Soak the mango slice in the brandy for as long as possible (overnight is good) in the bottom of a Champagne flute.

○ Just before serving, add the mango juice and the sparkling wine and stir gently, so as not to lose the bubbles.

○ Garnish with the cherry and serve immediately.

Above: Just add the sparkling wine and you have an instant welcome on the patio for your brunch-time guests.

Left: Cape Cream, a side-effect of international boycotts during South Africa's apartheid years.

Cape Cream

During the years when South Africa was boycotted because of her apartheid policies, several local drinks were invented to replace those no longer available. One was Cape Velvet Cream, a brandy-based cream liqueur that took the place of Bailey's Irish Cream. It makes a good cocktail ingredient.

ICE CUBES

TWO PARTS CAPE VELVET CREAM

ONE PART CAPE BRANDY

FRESH CREAM

GROUND CINNAMON

○ Place five or six ice cubes in a cocktail shaker, add the Cape Velvet and brandy and shake well.

○ Strain into a wine glass and carefully float the fresh cream on top.

○ Add a dusting of cinnamon before serving.

Above: North and south meet in a glass in this intriguing combination of French and African flavours.

Prickly Pear Syrup

Although prickly pears – those flat-leafed cactus plants with sweet, spiky fruit – are not indigenous to South Africa, they are seen everywhere in the country and their fruit is used to make a sticky sweet brown syrup sometimes used in local cocktails.

Use it sparingly or you end up with a very syrupy concoction.

CRUSHED ICE

TWO PARTS CANE SPIRIT

ONE PART FRESH LIME JUICE

ONE PART PRICKLY PEAR SYRUP

HALF A PART OF COINTREAU

- ❍ Place a scoop of crushed ice in a blender and add the ingredients.
- ❍ Blend for about five seconds, or until well mixed into a smooth slush.
- ❍ Pour into a lowball glass and serve.

asia and australasia

Modern travel and communications have brought the Far East ever closer to Western palates. Drinks like Midori and Sake, once available only to intrepid travellers, are now on sale across the globe. But remember, all drinks taste a little better when enjoyed in their countries of origin.

Gin and Tonic

In the far-flung outposts of the British Empire, malaria was a constant danger and quinine was often used as an antidote. It didn't take Her Majesty's servants long to discover that quinine tonic flavoured with a dash of gin made a dashed fine sundowner.

ICE CUBES

A GENEROUS MEASURE OF DRY GIN

TONIC WATER

A SLICE OF LEMON

○ Place three ice cubes in a tall glass. Splash in a liberal measure of gin and top up the glass with tonic.

○ Drop in a slice of lemon, twisted to release some of the zest.

○ Stir gently before serving.

Right: Gin and Tonic has been a favourite drink wherever the British forces have raised the imperial flag.

Cooch Behar

A fiery drink said to have been invented by the Maharajah of Cooch Behar in India.

ONE HOT RED PEPPER (COMPLETE WITH SEEDS)

ONE BOTTLE VODKA

TWO PARTS TOMATO JUICE

CRUSHED ICE

○ Steep the pepper in the vodka for two weeks.

○ Add one part of the pepper vodka to the tomato juice, pour over crushed ice and stir gently.

○ Serve in a lowball glass ungarnished.

Right: The Cooch Behar, a fiery creation to tempt brave oriental palates. Not for the faint-hearted.

Above: The Bombay was no doubt a popular drink in officers' messes from Rangoon to Rawalpindi.

The Bombay

Although it has an obviously Indian name, this drink has typically European ingredients and was probably invented by British officers during their occupation of India. The British had a reputation for hard drinking.

CRUSHED ICE

ONE PART BRANDY

ONE PART DRY VERMOUTH

HALF A PART OF SWEET VERMOUTH

A DASH OF CURAÇAO

A DASH OF PERNOD

A SLICE OF ORANGE

○ Place a scoop of crushed ice in a cocktail shaker and add all the ingredients except the orange slice.

○ Shake well and strain into a chilled lowball glass.

○ Garnish with the orange slice and serve.

Indian Cocktail

The cocktail tradition is growing in India, where it was previously considered a hangover from the days of British rule and shunned by the local population.

ICE CUBES

ONE PART SCOTCH WHISKY

ONE PART GIN

ONE PART DRY VERMOUTH

ONE TEASPOON ORANGE BITTERS

ONE TEASPOON COINTREAU

LEMON PEEL AND JUICE

○ Place several ice cubes in a bar glass and all the whisky, gin, vermouth, bitters and Cointreau.

○ Stir well and strain over ice cubes in a cocktail glass.

○ Squeeze the lemon over the drink and add the rind as garnish.

Above: The Indian cocktail – an elegant reminder of colonial days.

Burma Bridge Buster

War leaves casualties, but sometimes pleasanter reminders, too. This historic drink was allegedly created in Burma for the crews of the 490th Bombardment Squadron during World War II.

CRUSHED ICE

ONE PART PETER HEERING

TWO PARTS BRANDY

TWO PARTS LEMON JUICE

THREE PARTS LIGHT RUM

SUGAR SYRUP TO TASTE

○ Place a scoop of crushed ice in a blender and add all the ingredients.

○ Blend until smooth and strain into a cocktail glass.

○ Serve ungarnished.

Shanghai Lady

Purists claim the smell of a burning match adds a subtle, but important, dimension to this traditional drink, said to be served in the better Eastern establishments.

ICE CUBES

THREE PARTS GOLDEN RUM

ONE PART SAMBUCA

JUICE OF HALF A LEMON

TWO DASHES ANGOSTURA BITTERS

TWO TWISTS OF ORANGE ZEST

○ Place five or six ice cubes in a cocktail shaker and add the rum, Sambuca, lemon juice and Angostura bitters.

○ Shake well and strain into a chilled cocktail glass.

○ Pass the orange zest through the flame of a match two or three times and then drop it into the drink before serving.

Opposite left: Born in wartime, enjoyed in peacetime, the Burma Bridge Buster is a toast to airborne heroes.

Opposite right: Is your palate sensitive enough to taste the passing of a match flame in the Shanghai Lady?

Right: The Mikado – the perfect drink with which to toast the opening night of Gilbert and Sullivan's famous operetta.

Mikado

The popular British operetta, *Mikado*, created an imaginative Japan to delight the ears of British listeners. This Mikado is no less fictional, but pays tribute to a British musical tradition, rather than a Japanese reality.

ICE CUBES

A GENEROUS PART OF BRANDY

TWO DASHES OF ANGOSTURA BITTERS

TWO DASHES OF ORGEAT

TWO DASHES OF CURAÇAO

TWO DASHES OF NOYAUX

A MARASCHINO CHERRY

LEMON RIND

○ Place six ice cubes in a bar glass; add the brandy and dashes of orgeat, Curaçao and noyaux.

○ Stir together until well blended.

○ Strain into a cocktail glass and add a squeeze of lemon rind.

○ Serve decorated with the cherry.

singapore sling

THIS COCKTAIL BECAME a firm favourite of writers such as Joseph Conrad and Somerset Maugham. It was an elaborate concoction designed to please female drinkers, but was soon modified and enjoyed by cocktail lovers of both sexes. Here's a simplified and more practical version of the original, which contained no less than eight ingredients.

ICE CUBES

TWO PARTS DRY GIN

ONE PART CHERRY BRANDY

ONE PART FRESH LEMON JUICE

SODA WATER

A SLICE OF LEMON

A MARASCHINO CHERRY

❍ Place four ice cubes in a cocktail shaker and add the gin, cherry brandy and lemon juice.

❍ Shake well and strain into a highball glass.

❍ Top up with soda water and garnish with the slice of lemon and the cherry on a cocktail stick.

Opposite: The Singapore Sling was first served in Raffles Hotel in Singapore in 1915.

Above: The cool green colour of the Midori Dawn makes it the ideal cocktail for a poolside drink on a hot summer's day.

Midori Dawn

Midori is a Japanese liqueur based on muskmelon. It is bright green in colour and contains about 30 per cent alcohol. Midori adds both colour and flavour to a drink, making it an ideal cocktail ingredient.

ONE PART MIDORI

ONE PART VODKA

CRUSHED ICE

TONIC WATER

○ Mix equal parts of Midori and vodka in a bar glass.

○ Fill a lowball glass with crushed ice and pour the mixture over it.

○ Top up the glass with tonic water and serve.

Midori Sour

You can vary the ratio of sweet Midori to sour lemon juice to achieve the exact balance that's best for you. The proportions given here are for guidance only.

THREE PARTS MIDORI

TWO PARTS LEMON JUICE

ONE EGG WHITE

CASTER SUGAR TO TASTE

CRUSHED ICE

ONE RIPE RED CHERRY

○ Place all the ingredients in a cocktail shaker with a scoop of crushed ice.

○ Shake well and strain into a cocktail glass.

○ Garnish with the cherry on a cocktail stick.

Right: In the tradition of oriental taste, the Midori Sour creates a balance between sweet and sour.

Above: Suntory Sunset – in this pretty drink the red cherry sinks like sunset behind the frosty lychee mist.

Midori Sharp

Fresh grapefruit juice is an interesting cocktail ingredient that adds both sweetness and bitterness, often resulting in a crisply refreshing drink.

ONE PART MIDORI

FIVE PARTS FRESH GRAPEFRUIT JUICE

ICE CUBES

○ Stir together the Midori and grapefruit juice.

○ Fill a highball glass with ice cubes and pour the cocktail over them.

○ Serve ungarnished.

Suntory Sunset

Suntory is a Japanese brand of vodka, clear and intense, with a dry finish.

ONE PART SUNTORY VODKA

THREE PARTS LYCHEE JUICE

ICE CUBES

ONE RIPE RED CHERRY

○ In a bar glass mix the vodka and lychee juice by stirring gently.

○ Place three ice cubes in a cocktail glass and pour the liquid over them.

○ Garnish with the cherry on a cocktail stick.

Suntory Sour

Japan's Suntory company produces several kinds of liquor. Suntory whiskey is a popular drink all around the world and is naturally used in several Japanese cocktails.

CRUSHED ICE

THREE PARTS SUNTORY WHISKEY,

ONE PART FRESHLY SQUEEZED LEMON JUICE

A DASH OF WHITE CRÈME DE MENTHE

CASTER SUGAR TO TASTE

CLUB SODA

MINT LEAVES

○ Fill a highball glass almost to the top with crushed ice and pour in the whiskey, lemon juice, crème de menthe and caster sugar.

○ Stir gently until all ingredients are blended.

○ Fill the glass with club soda and garnish with a sprig of mint leaves.

Opposite bottom: The Midori Sharp is a bittersweet cooler for a hot summer's day.

Right: Japanese whiskey is respected by drinkers around the world. The Suntory Sour will please Eastern and Western drinkers alike.

Geisha

Sake, made from rice, is Japan's national drink, so it is not surprising that it appears in several Japanese cocktail recipes.

IICE CUBES

TWO PARTS BOURBON WHISKEY

ONE PART SAKE

A GENEROUS DASH OF SUGAR SYRUP

A SQUEEZE OF FRESH LEMON JUICE

○ Fill a bar glass with ice cubes.

○ Add the bourbon and sake, together with the sugar syrup and lemon juice, adjusting quantities of each to taste.

○ Stir well and strain into a lowball glass.

○ Add a squeeze of lemon zest and serve.

Right: East meets West in this interesting blend of flavours. You can balance the sweet and sour to suit your own palate.

Blushing Geisha

I have seen several versions of this elegant drink, some of which are enormously complicated and require two blenders running together. This is a much simpler version.

ICE CUBES

THREE FRESH STRAWBERRIES

A TEASPOON OF CASTER SUGAR

DASH OF LEMON JUICE

TWO PARTS SAKE

ONE PART CRÈME DE FRAISE DES BOIS (A STRAWBERRY LIQUEUR)

TWO PARTS CHILLED VODKA

○ Place five or six ice cubes in a cocktail shaker, add two strawberries, sugar and the lemon juice.

○ Use a cocktail spoon to crush the strawberries and blend in the lemon juice and sugar.

○ Add the sake, strawberry liqueur and vodka.

○ Shake well, and pour the entire contents, ice and all, into a lowball glass.

○ Serve garnished with a whole strawberry.

Right: The use of whole fruit always enlivens a cocktail and adds a freshness no extracts or preserved ingredients can match.

Sake Screwdriver

Another Sake-based drink, which is a Japanese adaptation of a popular western cocktail.

ICE CUBES

ONE PART SAKE

THREE PARTS FRESH ORANGE JUICE

A THIN SLICE OF FRESH ORANGE

○ Place three or four ice cubes in a highball glass and pour the Sake and orange juice over them.

○ Stir gently until properly blended.

○ Garnish with the slice of orange before serving.

Mount Fuji

Named after Japan's famous snow-capped mountain, this tasty drink will be at home in any country.

ICE CUBES

THREE PARTS GIN

ONE PART FRESH LEMON JUICE

ONE PART THICK CREAM

ONE EGG WHITE

HALF A PART OF CHERRY BRANDY

HALF A PART OF PINEAPPLE JUICE

MARASCHINO CHERRY (OPTIONAL)

○ Place five or six ice cubes in a cocktail shaker and add all the ingredients.

○ Shake well, fill a lowball glass with ice cubes and strain the cocktail over them.

○ Serve, garnished with the cherry if desired.

Above: A splash of cherry brandy adds a pretty pink blush to the misty Mount Fuji.

Opposite: The Sake Screwdriver gives a novel Eastern twist to an old classic.

Japanese Cocktail

This classical cocktail probably originated in America but is called the Japanese Cocktail for a reason now lost in the mists of time.

CRUSHED ICE

ONE PART ORGEAT SYRUP

ONE PART FRESH LIME JUICE

THREE PARTS BRANDY

A DASH OF ANGOSTURA BITTERS

LIME PEEL

○ Place a scoop of crushed ice in a cocktail shaker and add all the ingredients except for the lime peel.

○ Strain into a chilled cocktail glass and squeeze the lime peel over it to release the citrus oil.

○ Drop the peel in as garnish and serve.

Left: The squeeze of lime peel adds a subtle hint of zesty citrus oil to this delicate drink.

Japanese Fizz

Whiskey is a popular drink in Japan, where they produce several fine brands such as Suntory and Nikka. Ideally, this drink should be made using a Japanese whiskey, but it's almost as good with one from Scotland or America.

CRUSHED ICE

TWO PARTS JAPANESE WHISKEY

ONE PART RUBY PORT

HALF A PART OF LEMON JUICE

ABOUT A TEASPOON OF SUGAR SYRUP (OR TO TASTE)

CLUB SODA

ORANGE PEEL

A WEDGE OF FRESH PINEAPPLE

○ Place a scoop of crushed ice in a cocktail shaker and add the whiskey, port, lemon juice and sugar syrup.

○ Shake well and strain into a highball glass.

○ Fill with club soda and twist the orange peel over it to release the zesty oil.

○ Add the pineapple wedge and drop in the orange peel.

Right: Tangy citrus flavours make this a refreshing summer lunch-time drink with an alcohol content you can adjust to taste.

Saketine

Cocktails have become very fashionable in Japan, where they are often sold, ready-mixed, in cans. Sake, of course, plays a major role as a cocktail ingredient.

CRUSHED ICE

ONE PART COLD SAKE

ONE PART CITRUS VODKA

THREE PARTS CRANBERRY JUICE

COCKTAIL CHERRY

○ Place a scoop of crushed ice in a cocktail shaker and add the sake, citrus vodka and cranberry juice.

○ Shake well and strain into a cocktail glass.

○ Garnish with a cherry on a cocktail stick and serve.

Right: The cranberry juice gives this little gem a pretty pink glow and a tangy, fruity flavour.

Frozen Samurai

This is a popular Japanese drink, especially on a hot summer's day, when it's the adult equivalent of an ice-cream cone.

ONE SCOOP SOFT VANILLA ICE-CREAM

ONE PART KAHLUA

ONE PART AMARETTO

ONE PART BAILEYS IRISH CREAM

A SHORT DRINKING STRAW

○ Place the ice-cream in a large goblet, pour the other ingredients over it and serve. A short straw acts as a stirrer and can also be used to sip the melting ice-cream.

Right: The slow melting ice-cream makes the Frozen Samurai a drink to linger over. Why hurry such pleasure?

Fuji Sunset

Based on a popular Japanese liquor called Go-Shu Junmai, this is one of a whole host of new Japanese cocktails now appearing at cocktail bars in Japan's cities.

ICE CUBES

TWO PARTS GO-SHU JUNMAI

ONE PART MARASCHINO LIQUEUR

ONE PART FRESH LEMON JUICE

ONE PART FRESH ORANGE JUICE

A DASH OF GRENADINE

A COCKTAIL CHERRY

○ Place five or six ice cubes in a cocktail shaker, add all the ingredients and shake well.

○ Strain into a chilled Champagne saucer and serve with a cherry on the rim of the glass.

Right: A good drink should please the eye as well as the tongue, as the Fuji Sunset certainly does.

Eager Ninja

Sake is now being served chilled in cocktails instead of the traditional way of drinking it tepid. This cocktail can be made to look most colourful with its streaks of blue and red.

ICE CUBES

ONE PART SAKE

ONE PART MIDORI

ONE PART PINEAPPLE JUICE

A SPLASH OF BLUE CURAÇAO

A SPLASH OF RASPBERRY CORDIAL

COCKTAIL CHERRY

SLICE OF LIME OR LEMON

○ Place four or five ice cubes in a shaker and add the sake, Midori and pineapple juice.

○ Shake well and strain into a cocktail glass.

○ Now slide the blue Curaçao and raspberry cordial carefully down the sides of the glass to create streaks of colour.

○ Garnish with the cherry and slice of lemon or lime on the rim.

Right: The Eager Ninja can be made in a range of colours – or even streaks of colour – with imaginative use of the ingredients.

Bonsai Buddy

This unusual Japanese cocktail is made using a pre-mixed commercial sake cocktail as the main ingredient. Go-Shu Sparkling Sake cocktail has the scents of lychee and Muscat grapes. Using it in a cocktail adds new dimensions.

ICE CUBES

ONE PART GO-SHU SPARKLING SAKE COCKTAIL MIX

ONE PART SUNTORY WHISKEY

ONE EGG WHITE

ONE TEASPOON CASTER SUGAR

SODA WATER

SQUEEZE OF LEMON JUICE

○ Place six or seven ice cubes in a cocktail shaker, add the cocktail mix, whiskey, egg white and caster sugar.

○ Shake well until the egg white gives a silvery sheen.

○ Strain into a highball glass, top up with soda water to taste and squeeze the lemon over it before serving.

Left: The Bonsai Buddy is an interesting way to add complexity to a ready-mixed drink.

Right: If you enjoy your drinks bone dry, the Saketini may be exactly right for you.

Saketini

This is the Japanese version of the classic martini; the sake acts the part of the traditional vermouth in this case. One observer's comment was, 'it tastes like nothing, and that's the whole point'.

ICE CUBES

ONE PART SAKE

ONE PART VODKA

PINCH OF DRIED GROUND GINGER

SLICE OF CUCUMBER

○ Place four or five ice cubes in a shaker and add the sake, vodka and a pinch of ginger.

○ Shake well and strain into chilled martini glass.

○ Garnish with the slice of cucumber and serve.

Above: It takes all kinds of flavours to please the palates of the world; here we encounter the taste of green tea in the Zen Saketini.

Zentini

In this recipe, Zen is given a tangy lift by adding lime and citrus flavoured vodka.

ONE PART ZEN GREEN TEA LIQUEUR

TWO PARTS STOLI CITROS VODKA

A SPLASH OF FRESH LIME JUICE

ICE CUBES

○ Shake all the ingredients in a cocktail shaker with four or five ice cubes ice and strain into a martini glass.
○ Serve ungarnished.

Below: Lemon tea has long been an international favourite, so the lime and tea liqueur in the Zentini are natural companions.

Zen Saketini

This is yet another localized version of the old traditional martini and one not even James Bond would recognize as such.

Zen is a popular Japanese liqueur, flavoured with Japanese green tea.

ICE CUBES

ONE PART ZEN GREEN TEA LIQUEUR

TWO PARTS DRY SAKE

○ Shake both ingredients in a cocktail shaker with five or six ice cubes and strain into a chilled martini glass.
○ Serve ungarnished.

Zen Breeze

Here's a recently invented Japanese cocktail that adds a fruity note to the Zen green tea liqueur.

FRESH MINT LEAVES

ICE CUBES

ONE PART ZEN GREEN TEA LIQUEUR

TWO PARTS CRANBERRY JUICE

○ Place two or three mint leaves in the bottom of a cocktail shaker and crush them lightly with the handle of a knife.

○ Add four or five ice cubes, the green tea liqueur and cranberry juice and shake well.

○ Strain into a highball glass filled with ice and garnish with a sprig of mint leaves.

Left: All the senses are titillated in this Zen creation, using ice for its sound, mint for its scent and cranberries for colour and flavour.

Above: There's no question about the flavours gathered here: citrus added to citrus and decorated with citrus!

Yuzu Bath

Yuzu is a Japanese citrus fruit with a flavour somewhere between lemon and grapefruit. Shoshu is a distilled, clear spirit made from grain. The difference between it and sake is that sake is fermented, while shoshu is distilled.

FOUR PARTS SHOSHU

ONE PART ORANGE LIQUEUR

ONE PART CHILLED YUZU JUICE

ICE CUBES

SALT, MINT AND SUGAR TO FROST THE GLASS

SLICE OF LIME

SLICE OF ORANGE

○ Shake the shoshu, orange liqueur and yuzu juice with four cubes of ice in a cocktail shaker.

○ Strain into a cocktail glass that has had the rim frosted with a mixture of finely chopped mint leaves, salt and sugar.

○ Garnish with thin slices of lime and orange and serve.

Yuzu Bubble Bath

This drink is a taller version of the Yuzu Bath, this time with bubbles.

FOUR PARTS SHOSHU

ONE PART YUZU JUICE

ONE PART ORANGE LIQUEUR

ICE CUBES

SODA WATER

SLICE OF ORANGE

SLICE OF LIME

○ Place the shochu, yuzu juice and orange liqueur in a cocktail shaker and shake with five or six ice cubes.

○ Strain into a highball glass, top with Club soda and stir gently.

○ Garnish with lime and orange slices and serve.

Polynesian Pick-Me-Up

This gentle drink for the morning after is unlikely to cause any further damage. It relies on savoury flavours combined with tart, acid fruit juices to affect a cure. Look, nobody is saying this is a pleasant drink. It is, essentially, medicine.

CRUSHED ICE

ONE PART VODKA

FOUR PARTS FRESH PINEAPPLE JUICE

HALF A TEASPOON OF CURRY POWDER

A TEASPOON OF LEMON JUICE

TWO DASHES OF TABASCO SAUCE

CAYENNE PEPPER

○ Place half a cup of crushed ice and all the ingredients except the cayenne pepper in a blender.

○ Blend for about 10 seconds and pour it into a lowball glass.

○ Dust the surface lightly with cayenne pepper and drink it in a single, shuddering gulp.

Left: Yuzu Bubble Bath – almost any cocktail can be extended and turned into a long refreshing cooler by adding soda water to taste.

mai Tai

YOU'LL FIND VERSIONS of this classic cocktail in every drinks recipe book you open.

Apparently the name comes from the Tahitian expression, 'Mai Tai Roa Ae', which means

something like 'absolutely out of this world'. Like the famous Martini, this drink's

ingredients vary enormously from bar to bar.

ONE PART CURAÇAO

ONE PART APRICOT BRANDY

FOUR PARTS JAMAICAN RUM

JUICE OF HALF A FRESH LIME

A SPLASH OF SUGAR SYRUP

ICE CUBES

TWIST OF LIME PEEL

A CHUNK OF PINEAPPLE

A MARASCHINO CHERRY

○ Shake the liquid ingredients with ice in a cocktail shaker and strain into a chilled old-fashioned glass.

○ Garnish with the lime peel, pineapple and cherry.

Opposite: Mai Tai – could this be the 'real' one? Your bar tender probably knows differently.

Blue Lagoon

The Blue Lagoon is a cooling, ice blue summer drink. There's always something a little special about serving a blue drink.

CRUSHED ICE

THREE PARTS VODKA

ONE PART BLUE CURAÇAO

THREE PARTS PINEAPPLE JUICE

THREE DASHES OF GREEN CHARTREUSE

A SLICE OF PINEAPPLE

A COCKTAIL CHERRY (OPTIONAL)

○ Place half a cup of crushed ice in a cocktail shaker and add the vodka, Curaçao, pineapple juice and green chartreuse.

○ Shake well and strain into a lowball glass.

○ Serve decorated with a slice of pineapple, and a cocktail cherry if you feel like adding even more colour.

Tahiti Club

Probably a firm favourite with the members of
the Tahiti Club; now it's there for everyone to
enjoy. If you can make the various parts large
you can turn this into a superb summer cooler.

FOUR PARTS LIGHT RUM

ONE PART FRESH LIME JUICE

ONE PART FRESH LEMON JUICE

ONE PART PINEAPPLE JUICE

ICE CUBES

CRUSHED ICE (OPTIONAL)

A SLICE OF LEMON

○ Shake the liquid ingredients together with ice,
  then strain into a cocktail glass, or a tall glass
  filled with crushed ice.

○ Garnish with the slice of lemon.

Opposite: If you use a larger measure, you can turn the Tahiti Club
into a tall cooler, or even a summer punch for a whole party.

Above: Kava Cocktail – the peppery Kava plant adds a whole
new dimension to this orange-based drink.

Kava Cocktail

Kava is an interesting drink made from
the root of the Polynesian pepper plant,
sometimes crushed between two stones, and
sometimes (traditionally) chewed to crush it.

ONE PART KAVA

ONE PART LIGHT RUM

ONE PART DARK RUM

TWO PARTS FRESH ORANGE JUICE

A DASH OF GOMME SYRUP

CRUSHED ICE

○ Place all the ingredients in a cocktail shaker
  with a scoop of crushed ice.

○ Shake well and strain into a cocktail glass.

○ Serve ungarnished.

Waltzing Matilda

The 'Jolly Swagman' of the Australian song of the same name would probably have enjoyed tucking this refreshing summer drink into his tucker-bag. A lot better than drinking from the billabong, mate!

CRUSHED ICE

FOUR PARTS DRY WHITE WINE

ONE PART GIN

ONE PART PASSION FRUIT JUICE

HALF A TEASPOON OF CURAÇAO

SODA WATER OR GINGER ALE ACCORDING TO YOUR TASTE

ORANGE PEEL

○ Place a scoop of crushed ice in a cocktail shaker and add the wine, gin, passion fruit juice (you could use passion fruit cordial if the real thing is not available) and the Curaçao.

○ Shake briskly, then strain the contents into a highball glass.

○ Top up with the sparkling mixer of your choice and garnish with a twist of orange peel.

Left: Walzing Matilda as the name suggests, was invented in the dusty outback of Australia.

Plastered Possum

Midori may be Japanese in origin, but it has been welcomed as a cocktail ingredient by thirsty Australians.

ICE CUBES

ONE PART MIDORI

ONE PART GALLIANO

ONE PART COINTREAU

FOUR PARTS PINEAPPLE JUICE

ONE PART FRESH CREAM

○ Place six ice cubes in a cocktail shaker and add the Midori, Galliano, Cointreau and pineapple juice.

○ Shake well and strain into a goblet or cocktail glass.

○ Top with a layer of carefully poured cream. Alternately, add the cream before shaking, to end up with a smooth creamy drink.

Right: A whole range of liquor flavours adds up to a complex taste – and a hefty kick more akin to a mule than a possum.

Above: Every barman seems to have his own version of the Martini, so it should come as no surprise to find an Australian one.

Ned Kelly's Nightcap

Ned Kelly was the rough, tough Australian anti-hero featured in many Aussie folk tales. So we should not be surprised to find this a rough and tough drink, not for the faint-hearted.

ICE CUBES

ONE PART LIGHT RUM

ONE PART GOLD RUM

HALF A PART OF DARK RUM

HALF A PART OF ORANGE CURAÇAO

TWO PARTS OF ORANGE OR PINEAPPLE JUICE

○ Place six or seven ice cubes in a shaker and add all the ingredients.

○ Shake well and strain into any glass big enough to hold it all.

1763 Martini

The classic martini consists of gin and vermouth. Vermouth is a flavoured wine, so presumably some enterprising Australian outback barman simply substituted whatever wine was available for the vermouth and created his own version.

ICE CUBES

TWO PARTS BOMBAY SAPPHIRE GIN

ONE PART AUSTRALIAN RIELSING (OR ANY AVAILABLE WINE)

○ Place four or five ice cubes in a cocktail shaker, add the gin and wine and shake well for about 20 seconds, until well chilled.

○ Strain into a martini glass and serve.

Right top: Ned Kelly's Nightcap is said to be powerful enough to keep mosquitoes away for two nights after drinking it.

Right bottom: The Roo Rouser is claimed to be strong enough to raise a kangaroo from the dead.

The Roo Rouser

Kangaroos sometimes meet an untimely end on the rough roads of the Australian Outback. Local legend has it that one drink of this cocktail is powerful enough to raise a kangaroo from the dead.

ICE CUBES

ONE PART BRANDY

ONE PART BOURBON

ONE PART GIN

ONE PART RUM

ONE PART GINGER ALE

HALF A PART OF LIME JUICE

A DASH OF ANGOSTURA BITTERS

○ Place four or five ice cubes in a shaker, add all the ingredients and shake well before straining the result into a strong glass and serving.

Double K Crush

The kiwano, or horned melon, is unlikely to be available in any country apart from its native Australia, so if you're making this one elsewhere, substitute three very ripe strawberries for the melon.

ONE KIWANO MELON

TWO KIWI FRUIT (PEELED AND CHOPPED)

A GENEROUS HELPING OF VODKA

HALF AS MUCH COINTREAU

CRUSHED ICE

○ Cut the kiwano in half, scoop out the seeds and cut two thin slices for garnish.

○ Place the rest in a blender, together with the kiwi fruit and other ingredients, including a scoop of crushed ice.

○ Blend until smooth, pour into a glass and garnish with a melon slice. This recipe should make enough for two cocktail glasses.

Right: With all the fresh fruit in this tasty cocktail, you could almost claim it was a health food. It probably is.

Above: The almost-frozen Mary's Handcuffs is a natural choice for a hot summer lunch outdoors.

Above: The ingredients in the Dream Weaver have crossed oceans to meet in Australia.

Mary's Handcuffs

Maybe Mary became a bit unruly after trying this Australian drink and needed restraining. Who knows?

ONE PART LIME VODKA

ONE PART FRESH ORANGE JUICE

ONE PART LEMONADE OR MOUNTAIN DEW

○ All ingredients should be chilled in a freezer until slushy, but not frozen.

○ Into a cocktail glass, first pour the vodka then the orange juice and lemonade.

○ Stir gently and serve.

Dream Weaver

This drink has its origins in the Caribbean and Canada, but was invented in Australia.

ICE CUBES

THREE PARTS CANADIAN WHISKY

ONE PART LIGHT RUM

ONE PART FRESH ORANGE JUICE

ONE PART LEMONADE

○ Place four or five ice cubes in a shaker and add the whisky, rum and orange juice.

○ Shake well and strain into a tall glass filled with ice cubes.

○ Add the lemonade and stir gently before serving.

Glossary

As with any specialised field of activity, cocktail mixing and bartending in general have developed their own vocabulary. While we have tried to keep jargon to a bare minimum in this book, it's as well to know what people mean when they refer to a drink as being 'straight up' or a digestif. Here are some of the more commonly used cocktail terms.

Apéritif: A drink served before a meal to stimulate the appetite. Traditional apéritifs include fino sherry and brut champagne. Some cocktails are made dry for the same reason.

Bar syrup: A sweetening agent, usually made by mixing three parts sugar to one part water. A well-equipped bar always has a bottle of ready-made bar syrup handy.

Blend: In modern cocktail bars an electric blender has become standard equipment. It is particularly useful when fresh fruit is to be puréed as part of a drink. To blend a drink, run the machine for only about 10 seconds.

Dash: A dash of something is simply a small amount splashed into the glass. Usually very strong flavours, like bitters, sauces or syrups, are added in dashes.

Digestif: A small, usually quite sweet drink served at the end of a meal to aid digestion.

Flip: A flip is a short drink mixed with egg and sometimes sugar and shaken into a smooth froth. A single egg is often too rich for just one flip, and it is difficult to separate an egg into two, so it is easiest to make them two at a time.

Float: To pour a small amount of liquor or cream on top of a cocktail so it does not mix with the rest of the ingredients. This is often done by trickling it over the back of a spoon.

Frappé: A frappé is a drink made by pouring a sweet liqueur over crushed ice. It is served with a straw, so the melting ice and liqueur are sipped together from the bottom of the glass. See also 'Mist'.

Frosting: Glasses can be frosted by wetting the rim with water or egg white and dipping it into sugar, which then clings to the rim. Margaritas are traditionally served in glasses frosted with salt instead of sugar.

Jigger: A small measure used in making cocktails. The American jigger contains 1.5 ounces, or 42.3 cc. There are also one-ounce and two-ounce jiggers.

Mist: A straight (neat) alcoholic liquor poured over crushed ice. A mist is related to a frappé, which is a sweet liqueur poured over crushed ice.

Muddle: Herbs, such as mint, are sometimes muddled to release the juices and flavour. This is done by placing them at the bottom of a glass and crushing them to a smooth paste using a wooden pestle, so as not to scratch the glass. Sometimes bar spoons are made with a flat disc at the end of the long handle. This is designed to be used as a muddler.

Mulled: A drink served hot and usually enjoyed during winter. Originally drinks like ale and wine were warmed by plunging a hot poker into the tankard. As hot pokers are a rarity today, the drinks are simply warmed over a stove or hot plate.

Neat: Served without any mixer or ice. In Scandinavian countries, aquavit is often drunk neat. James Bond sometimes swigs his vodka neat.

On the rocks: Poured over ice cubes. Often a glass is filled to the top with ice cubes and the liquor is then trickled over

them. It serves a double purpose: it dilutes the liquor slightly and chills it.

Punch: A punch is a large drink made of liquor and fruits and served from a punch bowl at a large gathering. It's a sort of bulk-delivered cocktail.

Shake: To pour the ingredients into a cocktail shaker with some ice and shake it vigorously to ensure a good blend. The ice acts as a beater and dilutes it slightly.

Spiral: Sometimes a drink calls for a 'spiral' of orange or lemon peel. This is cut from the fruit in a long spiral and used to decorate and flavour the drink.

Straight up: Served without ice, usually in a tall glass.

Strain: After shaking or stirring a drink, you usually want to separate the liquid from the ice or peel or other solid ingredients. To do this, the drink is poured through a strainer. Good bars have specially designed strainers that fit over their shakers or mixing glasses.

Swizzle stick: A stirrer, sometimes made of silver, ivory or wood, but today mostly made of plastic. It acts as a decoration for the drink and can also be used to stir it from time to time. Many liquor companies provide swizzle sticks that bear the company logo or crest on the top.

Twist: A long piece of peel (usually citrus) that is twisted in the middle to release the tangy oil from the outer zest layer. It is then dropped into the drink as a garnish.

Zest: The very outside part of the citrus peel. It is obtained by cutting it off with a sharp knife or vegetable peeler. Zest does not include the soft white part (pith) of the skin.

Index

Most cocktails are illustrated on the same page as their recipe. Illustrations on other pages are indicated by *italic* references.